The 6.5 Practices of Moderately Successful Poets

JEFFREY SKINNER

———

THE 6.5 PRACTICES OF MODERATELY SUCCESSFUL POETS

———

A *Self-Help Memoir*

SARABANDE BOOKS
LOUISVILLE, KENTUCKY

Managing Editor
Sarabande Books, Inc.
2234 Dundee Road, Suite 200
Louisville, KY 40205

Library of Congress Cataloging-in-Publication Data

Skinner, Jeffrey.
 The 6.5 practices of moderately successful poets : a self-help memoir / Jeffrey Skinner.
    p. cm.
 ISBN 978-1-936747-27-6 (pbk. : alk. paper)
 1. Skinner, Jeffrey. 2. Poets, American—20th century—Biography. 3. Poetry—Authorship. 4. Poetry—Authorship—Humor. I. Title. II. Title: Six point five practices of moderately successful poets. III. Title: Six and a half practices of moderately successful poets. IV. Title: Practices of moderately successful poets.
 PS3569.K498Z46 2012
 818'.5403--dc23
 [B]
                          2011040876

Cover Image: *Poetry Reading* by Mick Stevens.
Cover and text design by Kirkby Gann Tittle.

Manufactured in Canada.
This book is printed on acid-free paper.

Sarabande Books is a nonprofit literary organization.

The Kentucky Arts Council, the state arts agency, supports Sarabande Books with state tax dollars and federal funding from the National Endowment for the Arts.

for my students

Reader, I think proper, before we proceed any farther together, to acquaint thee that I intend to digress, through this whole history, as often as I see occasion, of which I am myself a better judge than any pitiful critic whatever; and here I must desire all those critics to mind their own business . . .

—Henry Fielding

All of old. Nothing else ever. Ever tried. Ever failed. No matter. Try again. Fail again. Fail better.

—Samuel Beckett (*Worstward Ho*)

TABLE OF CONTENTS

Introduction to the Preface

I don't mean anything by it. I don't have anyone in mind. No one in particular. Most of my friends are poets.

Poetry is the best thing in the world. Poets who write poetry, and then keep writing it, are *very* brave. Not as brave as soldiers, or policemen, or firemen, or people who work with the disabled, or in nursing homes, or with Alzheimer's patients, not as brave as Alzheimer's patients, or people who do the same crappy job every day for forty years so their kids can have a better life, or people who lose a limb, or people who are paralyzed and choose to go on with a positive attitude, or motorcyclists, or gang members, or boxers, or women in prison, or electricians, but brave—poets are brave, nonetheless.

I mean it.

I wrote this book for poetry and for poets. That is, for you. I love the brave people who write poetry, and then keep writing poetry. In this book, starting in the preface coming up very soon, I seem at times to be making fun of poets.

Dear Reader, Dear Poet: I *am* making fun of poets.

But I myself am a poet who writes poetry and keeps writing poetry, and I am included in the bravery and the fun. The making fun of. For I am often the target of my own satire. And I am not making fun of *poetry*, italicized.

Dear Reader, Dear Poet: when times get rough in this book I hope you will think of me as another poet, another *kind* of poet—Don Rickles.

I kid, I kid because I love. I love you.

Preface

Yes. They walk among us and we never know, never suspect. They get government grants, they teach at the local college or university, they drop their children off at the Montessori school. They enjoy movies, music, dance—maybe even a sport (basketball or baseball, yes; football or boxing, no)—many of the things regular people enjoy. They drive Hondas or Toyotas or Volvos. Or, they don't drive at all. They like travel and ethnic foods. They like wine, and locally brewed beer. They adore gossip about other poets.

They like talking to intelligent people, people who also *do* something. Intellectuals windy with thought alone, not so much. They like hanging with artists and musicians and architects. They like alcohol, yes, and sometimes too much.

They like being with their own kind—other moderately successful poets, but only for limited periods. For them hell is a locked auditorium just about to host a literary awards ceremony, the joint crowded with other poets, all competing for the same prizes, grants, publications.

They mill, sweat, and drink.

Mostly solitary creatures, moderately successful poets roam the forests and meadows of artists' colonies in search of metaphor, and short-term affairs with composers and/or visual artists.

In heaven, all poets would have a constellation of their own.

And it's true, we are pitiable in the same measure we are, at times, pompous.

We live hearing an ostinato of low-grade anxiety. In addition to the mortal wonderings of middle-aged truck drivers, accountants, doctors, and doormen, we add our own specially flavored, unanswerable riddles: have we given too much to our art, or have we given too little? What about our family, have we given enough of ourselves to them? To the rest of life?

We are big-hearted and petty, direct and devious, sober and mad, confident and terrified. Sorrowing, and *happy*—whole moments at a time!

In short, moderately successful poets are like everyone else. Just, maybe more so.

Poetry is a mug's game, Eliot said. And yet in spite of all I have stacked up against my tribe, in spite of a "professional" life that inevitably includes more than our share of rejection, disappointment, humiliation, in spite of the fact that we have taken to warning students off the path—*become an engineer, or a lawyer, a businesswoman, find a little happiness for Christ's sake*—we go on writing poetry.

And now I will tell you the secret.

Moderately successful poets have one recompense that more than rights the balance of unfairness, that keeps them hoping, and dreaming words, long after the realization that what they do will not lead to fame or money in this world, nor immortality in the next:

They get to write poetry.

That's it, really. Sometime early in life moderately successful poets discovered *the word* and felt their DNA rise up and lean toward it like iron filings to a magnet.

It was not ambition that brought us to poetry, but *recognition*.

We are capable of doing other things, have done other things. Many of us have had other careers, or have them still. But for moderately successful poets, nothing compares with the moment of writing a poem, when the words are coming freely, gifts from the dreamy beyond. Poetry has ruined them for any other occupation.

And it is not even an occupation! Poetry is *not* a job, career, avocation, hobby, necessity, luxury, etc.

Well, what *is* it then? It's an art, sure. But an art made of words—which happen also to be the medium of marketing, politics, journalism, and religious dogma. Why can't poems make sense, our Uncle Don says. And we squirm, or apologize, or condescend, or fix another drink. There is nothing to say, really.

Doesn't matter. At some point we were struck on the head by the poetry brick. We spent our youth wandering in that lovely daze. Then life happened, as it does to all. We were hit by more bricks. We should have awoken then to pragmatism. But it was too late. Poetry had become our way of seeing, our mode of consciousness, our gateway between the physical and whatever lies beyond. It had become, somehow, our chief delight, and our being.

This life, the poet Greg Orr says, *like no other.*

Introduction

I have written this book to give some sense of the life of an American poet in the late twentieth century and extending into the twenty-first. I mean also to give the reader interested in writing poetry some guidance in aspects of the *craft*, if such a thing actually exists (more on that later).

This book is for all who may be curious about the actual, as opposed to, yes—the fantasy—life of a contemporary American poet.

I also aim my words at the isolate reader, the ones just beginning to be transformed by poetry, who may not have anyone to share with them the strange, newly forming sense of wonder and possibility inside a poem.

In order to do this I have employed a number of approaches, including charts and graphs, burlesques, jokes, lists, impersonations, and stories from my own life. The life of poetry is inseparable from the poet's life, Skinner says. This may not be a truth for all, but it is true for Skinner and, I believe, most poets.

And although I make no claim that *my* life as a poet has been exemplary, typical, or admirable, I do think there may be something peculiarly American about my story.

———

I was raised in Levittown, Long Island, New York, which at the time was a working-class bastion with young dads and moms just starting out, the dads back from the war, able to buy their Levitt house because of Levitt's genius and the G.I. Bill.

In our home there was a Bible and *The Reader's Digest*, maybe an encyclopedia my mother bought in installments at the supermarket. Everyone I knew, child and grownup alike, would have said poets were men, more than likely Englishmen, who died long ago. They might just as well have been characters in a fairy tale. No one in my family had been a "writer," or could even imagine what that might mean. Though I myself was an avid reader, I didn't think of writing as something to *do*. I had no curiosity about writers. I wanted stories of adventure and magical transformation; the Mowgli jungle stories, for example, were my obsession for a memorable period. For me books had a presence like trees and animals—they were there as givens. The idea of authorship did not occur.

But the Yankees, on the other hand, were real, *and* legend—it was the era of Mickey Mantle, Yogi Berra, and Roger Maris. Yankee Stadium was around forty minutes away.

Levittown was filled with kids, a billion of them, it seemed. It was the Baby Boom and wherever I looked there were others my size and approximate shape. We played stickball and triangle in the streets, we swam in the communal pools.

Little League, competitive swimming, model cars and airplanes. Hula Hoops, Herman and the Hermits, boomerangs, Red Skelton, go-go boots, transistor radios.

The World's Fair came to Flushing Meadows. I went eight times. Love them Belgian Waffles, the penpal from Japan I found by typing into a marvelous machine. The rides, especially the smooth trip on rails with tiny Lucite future cities on either side, lit from beneath, glittering in the velvet dark. It's a small, small world.

I was shy but big for my age. Bullies left me alone. I liked reading more than sports, otherwise they would have gotten to me. My friends and I used to trade punches on the arm riding the school bus, for the high entertainment value. I will never forget how I dreaded John Immel's turn to hit me. Man, that kid had guns.

My teacher in first grade, Miss Miranti, let me take a clock apart, off in a corner, by myself. I loved her.

I sucked at football, but loved fall, the smell of burning leaves, the dry, brisk wind as I took to the field for windsprints. I even liked the gummy taste of my mouthguard, a rubbery, waxy flavor that, by the end of practice, would inevitably be mixed with the copper of my own blood.

Every Fourth of July some kid in the neighborhood blew off a portion of a digit, sometimes a whole finger. Ronnie Delano practiced drums in his attic room. The whole neighborhood could hear his twilight thumping. We rode bikes, wagons, scooters—everything—without helmets. We spent countless hours outside and never told our parents what we'd done. They never asked. All the kids got spanked, and neighbors were allowed to cuff you if your parents weren't around and you got out of line. We never used seatbelts. There were no seatbelts. We played knights in junkyards with shards of rusted metal for swords.

How did we not die, all of us?

We loved cars and baseball cards and packing ice inside snowballs to throw at passing cars. All this seemed endless, so we didn't spend much time thinking about the rest of our lives. If we did we would quickly say we wanted to be cops or firemen or coaches, or carpenters, like our dads. This was the boys, of course. I don't know what the girls wanted, or thought.

Big, shiny, grownup Manhattan was a bus ride away, and I often visited there to see the wonders, but it might have been on another planet. Everything was made of concrete. It was the place my grandparents sailed to from across the Atlantic and had to stop and get checked in before they could start their new life in America. It was where my dad worked, and where most of the dinosaur bones and other *very important things of the world* were stored. It was an island, and I lived on another, even bigger island, right nearby. There was ocean all around.

This is what I came from.

1. Protects Talent

Talent is insignificant. I know a lot of talented ruins. Beyond talent lie all the usual words: discipline, love, luck, but most of all, endurance.

—James Baldwin

What Is Talent?

One of my academic colleagues once announced to me that he "believed in talent," as if it required a reluctant species of faith in things unseen, and he was feeling generous. I was surprised, since I'd been teaching poetry for a number of years and thought that poetic talent was more or less self-evident. Out of a beginning workshop of twenty, after the first or second exercise, I would generally find at least one student handing in pieces that had a freshness and ease with language, a startling honesty, an offbeat beauty, that were to me the hallmarks of talent. Perhaps at first these elements would be present only in a line here and there, or an image, a scrap of vernacular speech. Or they would be buried in the usual gummy mass of cliché and conventional tropes of "poetry" that had hardened in the public mind.

Nevertheless, traces of the real were unmistakable. I'd be plowing through student work from Intro to Creative Writing, a generally cheerless task, when an unexpected line would suddenly make me laugh out loud, or cause a dry catch in the back of my throat or the hair to rise on the back of my neck.

These involuntary responses were the giveaway: I'd stumbled across *poetry* . . . the student had bumped into *poetry*. Maybe the student had done so by design, more likely by accident. Whatever. It was a rare and celebratory occasion.

But, if I *kept* on finding such moments in any student's work, I would call it *talent*. And I would not hesitate to call that student *gifted*.

3

The Part That Learns Without Effort

I hadn't taught the students to do such things—they came to class bearing the capacity. Part of my job, I considered, was to point out such lines, such moments, to say, here, look at *this*, isn't *this* interesting? To get them to feel the peculiar energy in a line of poetry they had written, how familiar *and* how oddly alien at once, how detached from the ordinary "self."

Try to follow the strange aptness of what you've said, I'd say. Pick up that line like a string and follow it back to the source, the big ball of string, wherever that is.

Bring me back more of the same.

Rigor, Precision

I love how students come to me with those dilated, belladonna eyes after discovering poetry, the astonishment and excited hope that poetry has opened. I know exactly how they feel, and I confirm their excitement with the reflection of my own. I give them the names and books of other poets I know will feed that fire. I assure them that no moment spent reading poetry is wasted. I tell them their parents won't help in this business and will probably become anxious if they try to enlist their interest. I implicitly offer myself as *in loco parentis*, a kind of wacky, renegade, but still trustworthy dad. You can give *me* your wildness, your poetry, I say. I'll take it seriously, I'll dig it. I won't say, *That's nice dear, now get back to work.*

I don't tell them anything I don't believe.

I do all this within the institutional structure and, even though I encourage students to trust the reality of the post-adolescent storm of strong feeling, as well as their awakening to what language has hidden from them all these years, I am no guru and will not set up as one. I don't want followers—too messy, too dangerous, too . . . silly. Besides, I looked into the purchase of one of them giant egos, years ago. It's way more than I want to spend.

Students, I say, we have to live in the world as it is, with all its drudgery and material necessity. Don't sneer at the world outside poetry. That's where most people, including most of the kindhearted ones, live.

Then I detail the costs and risks of the artistic life, the unpredictability, the real fear of failure, the selfishness and bulletproof ego absolutely necessary for the job. I tell them to do *any* other thing with their lives if they can.

And, after knowing the costs, if they still insist on giving themselves to poetry—*Go!* I say.

Providence has a soft spot for poets and drunks. I know this as fact, from personal experience. And I will go with them a little way on their journey. Partly because it's my job. But also because their enthusiasm restores *me* and keeps at bay, for a time at least, that old Wordsworthian sadness—that place where poets end.

Students are after all just beginning, in gladness.

But I do not forget that rigor and precision are part of the real world of the arts, as much as science or business or any other human sphere. I owe it especially to my gifted students not to coddle, or to pretend that talent will be all. I want to temper their awakening to the *word*, to sharpen and focus their beautiful enthusiasm.

In general I'd encourage what remained after I'd taught them to pound the crap out of their little clay balls of language. I was not mother or father, I was not their friend. I *was* some kind of freak who had read thousands of poems, tens of thousands of lines of poetry and, having written a somewhat lesser amount myself, come back to tell them, having gone through many years of being harsh with myself.

I could do students the favor of lifting to consciousness the varied sources of clichés and received bits of language and thought. I could help in unmasking the censor that barred access to the place where observation, feeling, and language are one. I could tell them how intimate I was with my own failures, past and continuing.

I could show them, through study of published poems, how essential precision in language is to opening their inner states to others. Tool and die makers are accustomed to working with exceedingly low tolerances, and if we're talking about something like airplane parts, for example, the quality of their making has a direct impact on human safety. Okay, your poem probably won't kill anyone. But language can be as hard as metal, and words do have consequences. You want to be as insistent on fit and finish in your poems as the tool maker we unknowingly trust, stepping on the plane.

How you say goes a long way in determining how the reader receives. You want to communicate with other humans, I say, or you wouldn't write poems. Always then there is one who insists: *But I'm writing for myself, really.* . . . Oh yeah? Dear Reader, Dear Poet, if you're writing for yourself your audience will always be too lenient, too quick to reply, *Yes, yes, I know exactly what you mean!* even if your words on paper do *not say* anything near what you mean.

These things I can do. I can try and do. My own way, my style, is brio with a bit of absurdist humor, respect for each student's dignity, and zero patience for the 99% crap we spew (myself included) when we claim to be writing poetry. Talent can take it. If it can't, there's always law, or real estate, or politics. The sweet meat of poetry needs a good dab of wasabi—*yes!* I want to burn my students' tongues, in a flavorful, humorous way, before the world does it with boiling water.

Unfairness

My blunt honesty is nothing compared to what even my most gifted students would encounter when they left school. There is no less democratic or compassionate field than that of "professional art," whether the art is visual, performance, or writing. Cuts in the applicant pool (*any* of the applicant pools) are made for the most part quickly and with surgical detachment. Explanations are not offered. Next please.

A moderately successful life in the arts requires blazing, unmistakable talent, or a mix of some degree of talent and the qualities James Baldwin enumerates. Also, as Baldwin says and Charles Bukowski so eloquently agrees, *luck counts.*

So it is a meritocracy, with waivers.

It is an irony, of course, that most artists, when you make the mistake of asking them about civic matters, will almost invariably proclaim the virtues of tolerance, inclusivity, cooperation, and working for the common good. These same qualities vanish when artists, writers, performers are chosen for parts, or shows, or book publication, or record deals, etc. But maybe even Simon Cowell talks this way when he is not considering investing his own money or reputation in a new singer or group.

The gatekeepers of the arts are all Simon Cowells.

I have worked in business and in the academy, and in those domains (and, I suspect, also in law and medicine) there is always a place for mediocrity, sometimes a warm and cozy place. But in the arts you have to be *really good* just to be invited in from the cold. And then you better *keep on* being really good, or your ass will be summarily kicked back into February.

I'm speaking generally. It's not a pure meritocracy. There is no pure anything, and art is *more* subjective, and therefore more definitionally impure, than almost any other field.

Everyone has his list of untalented posers who have published x number of useless books. Pandering works, if you're good at it. Poets who are "popular" (within the tiny arena of poetry) and sell a comparatively large number of books may or may not be artistically respectable. Sometimes book sales are due to the accessibility of the poetry itself, and a larger, Garrison Keillorian "nonprofessional" audience bumps sales figures. Sometimes the opposite: the book is aggressively obscure, or trendy in some other way, and book sales rise because young poets hunger for the cutting edge.

And it must also be said that there exists today a hierarchy of "kinds of artists" who are deemed automatically interesting (or not) because of something about them, some biographical detail, or trauma, or scrap of historical legacy fate has handed them—their "identity"— which has little to do with the art. It's tiresome, but also part of life as it is.

I know that saying this will raise objections, accusations. I will not engage the whole, huge argument. Besides, global language is for global politics, not poetry. I will say that it once seemed possible to talk about poetry as *poetry*. What do I mean by this? Dear Reader, thanks for the question.

A few decades ago (*Lord have mercy*) when I read every new issue of *Poetry* magazine because it was interesting, I remember a review of the last book by one of my favorite poets, John Berryman. The reviewer remarked on a tone, new in Berryman, that colored the book. It was ominously dark and, for the reviewer, prefigured Berryman's suicide. But the review went on to say the tone did not, overall, detract from the *quality* of the poems. He went on to quote one short poem in its entirety, and the next sentence of his review was, "The poetry is superb."

We would be hard-pressed to find such a simple, declarative sentence in a poetry journal today.

Sometimes it seems that all of postmodern art has been (is) various embodiments of the shadow argument about *what art is*, and *who gets to say what art is*. This has been largesse for the cultural critic and the academic. For the intelligent, nonprofessional reader of poetry this argument, while it has its charms, is of limited interest. For the contemporary poet it has resulted in a radical opening of the possibilities for what poetry might include, as well as an explosive undoing of the word "meaning." This is exciting, sure. But it also has had the effect of flattening the landscape of poetry, so that there are no longer any mountains or valleys, and the *best* terrain means only that place some individual or group *prefers* to live.

There is no authoritative person or thing to appeal to. No one *here* can be better than any other *there*.

Necessary Selfishness

Cultivate necessary selfishness. The world—even the literary world—will ask you to do everything except write a new poem. That, you must ask of yourself.

—Jane Hirshfield

Because there are always far more important things to do than write a poem (do taxes, cook dinner, call Mom), I have to induce in myself the illusion of temporary freedom from those things.

—Chase Twichell

But I have said no to committees, opportunities, parties, dinners, friends, etc., in order to say Yes to poems. I do not regret the choices, though sometimes I regret the poems!

—David Baker

Because I am so easily distracted by the matters of domestic life—and will put anyone or anything ahead of my writing—I need to go away from home, where I can be completely alone.

—Cleopatra Mathis

Selfishness has helped a lot over the years. That is, if you have a spouse and a family, the claiming of time and space to work. Of course, as we the selfish know, there's a cost for selfishness, but that's another matter, perhaps the stuff of memoir.

—Stephen Dunn

Dear Reader: Enough said?

Life and Work

After I'd begun to publish my poems some and finally had a few friends who were also poets I stayed with one such friend overnight while en route to an artists' colony. I can't tell you his name but his initials were *Michael Waters*. It was summer and Michael taught college and so I asked him what he'd been up to in June, the previous month. He said he and his wife had traveled to Thailand and found a beautiful beach where you could stay dirt cheap but live like royalty. They rented a thatched cottage on the beach the whole month for an embarrassingly small amount of money, and enjoyed the ocean and the weather and the sweet Thai people. And, Michael added, he had actually managed to do some work.

Why? I asked. What kind of work? He looked at me suspiciously then as if to discern whether or not I was fucking with him. It must have been obvious from my expression that I was not—that I was serious, because he answered, *I was writing poems, you idiot. I was working on* poems.

Writing poems was *work?* Hmmmmm. . . .

If you grew up working-class, as I did, around other working-class people, your attitude toward *work* was that it was something one did for money, to pay the bills. It was necessary and honorable, work, and one's self-respect depended on it. I was raised by parents who had lived through the Depression, after all. To have a job of any kind was a very good thing. Every job came with its own built-in dignity.

But work and money had a direct relationship: you did one and then got the other. There was no requirement that your work be especially "meaningful," to you or to anyone else. Of course, if you were working on a road crew spreading asphalt then when you finished the job there was that new road you had helped to make; and roads *were* meaningful.

But this is a kind of archaic meaning of the word *meaning*. The meaning of *meaning* has shifted, particularly as used by the educated classes. The idea, for example, that back in the day one of us kids might hold out for a summer job that contributed to social justice, or the environment, or for an internship that would be *relevant* to one's later career, was unheard of. Literally. That was for another era—coming soon but still at that moment invisible. If we had even been able to put such an idea into words (*Cutting lawns is swell, Dad, but I really want to see what I can contribute to social justice*) it would have been dismissed out of hand as gobbledygook. If we had then been so crazy as to persist, our parents would have stopped what they were doing and studied us with sharp eyes. Then they would have labeled such nonsense as a *fancy excuse*, and ordered us to get up off our asses and find some lawns to cut, or shopping carts to fetch from the local A & P parking lot.

Or, to ask Uncle Gene if we could join him for the summer in his roofing business, and of course thank him profusely on the off chance he said yes. Yeah, yeah—that's a good idea. Go on over and see your Uncle Gene, *this* weekend. And don't let me hear from him if you do get the job that your roofing is anything less than *excellent*. You will *not* embarrass this family. You *will* make us proud. And I know you don't like Aunt Alice, because—*you say*—she has a "funny smell." Tough luck. You just better be the soul of politeness and act the gentleman whenever you're over by her. Are you *listening* to me?

So from the time I was around fifteen I did a string of different jobs, including fetching carts at the A & P *and* helping Uncle Gene roof houses for a summer. I drew the line at mowing lawns; doing our own lawn was misery enough. I was able to maintain this low standard because there was always an even crappier job available if I wanted it.

At some point in the Levittown years my father got restless and tired of working for the government and quit his job as Chief Investigator for the Nassau County Board of Supervisors and went out on a thin financial limb and bought a private investigative firm in Connecticut. Now that he was working only for himself and his family, *and* owed a substantial amount to the bank, it was essential that he establish himself in a new city, build the business, and succeed. My father had always worked long hours but now he seemed to do nothing but work and we rarely saw him. He was not about to fail. Besides, he loved to work. And now he was working for himself and could make his own rules and everything rose and fell on his doing. Which was just as he wanted.

It didn't hurt that he was athletic and good-looking and the strong, quiet type, the type who really could handle dangerous jobs involving dangerous people. Word of mouth spread and business grew. In fairly short order he no longer had to go knocking on lawyers' doors for work—they came to him. At the time my father looked like a young Lee Marvin. Women were attracted to him, men admired him and wanted to hang with him. The investigative business grew to several times the size it was when he took over.

From then on, although I occasionally had other jobs, I worked for him while going through high school and college. Even after that, when I had entered my twenties and was seduced by poetry and promptly entered a foggy decade of bewilderment about how exactly one is to reconcile love of art with the necessity of paying for rent, food, booze, and books, I worked for my father.

There were advantages. Because my father had lots of cases, and because of the odd hours called for by surveillance, I could pick and choose when I worked. And it paid well, at least for someone my age. And you weren't stuck in the same place doing the same thing over and over.

But it was still a *job*. It was working for my father.

Later in life and to this day when I tell people I was a private investigator they get all wide-eyed with excitement, *every one of them*—beautiful young women to middle-aged insurance agents to academics. *Did you carry a gun?* they ask. *Did you ever get into a fight?* They lean in to hear the answer, they nearly vibrate on their seats. *C'mon, tell us, what was it* like?

I wish I had realized all that time I was working as an investigator

14

what effect, what power the mere idea of *private investigator* had on nearly everyone, at least everyone outside the business of law enforcement, and its subsidiaries. I could have harnessed that iconic force, that irresistible stereotype, to impress women and intimidate men. The effect was often not so impressive and welcoming when I was actually working as an investigator and trying to extract information from some reluctant subject. Many of the hard types I dealt with viewed what I did as slightly below (slightly above?) that of street cop. In fact, even though I had the proper license and an ID card to match, I often lied about who I was and what I was after, because it was a better bet to get people to open up.

But for those I wasn't trying to con for the sake of information, the years of movie and TV images had made my profession impossibly romantic. It would have been heady stuff for a young man, especially one without much confidence in himself or his semiopaque future.

If I only knew . . .

Instead I thought what I did for a living was just work. It was a lot of boring courthouse record checks and doing background interviews for lawyers and corporate human resource executives. Or shadowing cheating husbands or wives and taking pictures of them when they met their lover at some low-life motel. Or sitting hours in the car down the street from some con man who was supposedly hurt so badly in a job-related accident he couldn't work, and yet there he was—teetering on the roof of his house as he twirled the TV antenna, his wife yelling to him through the window when the reception improved.

Camera here: click, click. Gotcha, asshole.

Odious people. I was glad my photographs would nail these dicks. Of course, I was young then and there is no more bulletproof morality than that of a twenty-something striding through life without temptation, who is in fact without temptation because everything he wants he allows himself to take, and he has not yet arrived at the inevitable place where penalties come due.

15

No, I wasn't conscious then of the images that attach to professions, or the power such images hold for others. To me the cool thing was writing. In bars I'd be mum about my PI work, and instead go on and on about *Prufrock* or Berryman's *Dream Songs*. If only I'd shut up about poetry and used the cachet of what I actually did for a living, I would have gotten laid much, much more. Which was the objective when I held forth on poetry to some poor unsuspecting woman. If only I'd known I could have introduced myself by opening her hand palm up on the bar and merely placing in it my ID— *Jeffrey Skinner, Private Investigator*. I would have had more perks, more status, more respect, more of the things everybody wants.

I was such a fool.

The older I got, of course, the more complex my life (second wife, children, teaching job, house, etc.) became, the less energy I had. So there was a necessary concurrent increase in the amount of discipline that would enable me to support the life *and* the poetry.

This is what I'm getting at: I'm lazy. I have only practiced the minimum amount of discipline necessary to live and write. And though I was for a time a willing anchorite and did give up a great deal for poetry, I was not willing to give up everything—I wanted a real mate, children, a job I could believe in. So I may not be the one for the best advice about how to balance the life and the work. This is one of the main reasons to study with an older poet—to find out how the hell to manage the balancing act.

And yet in spite of my disabilities I think I can say I have enjoyed (wrong word) a career as a moderately successful poet. I have found at least a working balance in my life. It was arrived at through trial and error, it has not been consistently applied, it is forever in constant flux. But, somehow it has worked for me.

So here are some ways, abstracted directly from my own experience and that of other contemporary poets I respect, that you might order your life so as to have the maximum amount of time for writing (and reading), without giving up other significant dimensions of that life, and/or compromising a minimal moral code:

- Carve out specific, reliable times in your week for writing, and let nothing short of a medical emergency for you or your immediate family interrupt or suspend such times.

- Consider the expense of books, computers, and office supplies part of the cost of your "business." If you have to cut your budget, do so in other areas. Give in to the pleasure of periodic visits to stationery stores. When you write well, reward yourself with beautiful notebooks, boxes of fine-point roller pens, a computer upgrade, a buying spree at your local independent bookstore.

- Since the world will give you so few of them, you should continuously add to the preceding list of rewards which you will give yourself for finishing a poem, a book, or for publishing well, or for merely staying in the room with a piece of blank paper for a given period of time. As each of us has different affinities, you will over time compile your own list of appropriate rewards. Mine include such things as iTunes downloads, new clothes, or additions to any one of my collections of custom-made folding knives, cast-iron toys, art deco lamps, and vintage fountain pens.

- If you are not writing, don't immediately call it tragic. It may be you are not supposed to be writing at that moment. We don't have to write all the damn time (see the chapter *Takes the Long View*).

- When you are awake, be fully awake. Try to be present and alert even when in the midst of boring or painful tasks—at the DMV, or the dentist, or in conversation with your mother. This *habit* of intense, loving alertness will increase the volume of your life, making more reality available to your writing, and more sharpness in the writing. On the other hand, when you play or sleep, just play, just sleep.

➡ Get rid of all your notions of how or when poems are to be written. Discard all superstitions. Even though you set aside particular times for writing, remain open to the possibility that a poem can happen in the middle of the dance floor, or on the subway, or while working out, or eating dessert. Keep that notebook handy.

➡ Keep the writing and the business parts (submissions, grant applications) of your poetry life *separate*. The business part should be done with even more discipline and detachment than the writing. Part of you must hire on as the work's secretary, and as secretary your job is to keep the poems in circulation—in the face of the wider world—even at those times when the composer in you is dejected and discouraged. Schizophrenia is a necessary adjunct to the writer's life.

➡ Like the Zen master, have your *yes*, and your *no*. Become adept at turning down invitations (Requests? Demands?) that take away from your writing time without adding to your breadth of life. For example, I may decide to forgo some writing time in order to see a new production of a Pinter play, but I will not give up one minute to be part of a Committee for the Advancement of Really Important Committee Work.

➡ Give yourself goals; have a plan. Say to yourself, during blissful extended periods of writing, *You, Jeff, must fill x number of pages with words per day.* Or, that you will have a first draft done of a new piece by such and such a date. Or, that you will edit a manuscript by this particular date. Give yourself contingent rewards and punishments—e.g., *If I finish the x number of pages in forty minutes I am done, and can go out and play, as is my wont. If I do not produce x pages in the allotted time I must stay at it until I do, no matter what hours may pass.* Though both are good, I like the self-imposed arbitrary goals even more than those given me by others. "Arbitrary" is the key word; satisfying simple quantitative requirements frees

18

the writing mind from anxiety about results, and opens it to range freely in the liminal, where the good stuff happens.

➥ Make use of artists' colonies. These wonderful places give the writer that blissful uninterrupted writing time we all crave, in an environment of low pressure, surrounded by others, all trying to do the same difficult thing. It's not only the time these places grant, but also the sense they confer that making poems is *important business*; hard to get this elsewhere in the world. Of course, in order to make use of the two-week to three-month periods awarded by MacDowell or Yaddo, or the other colonies, the poet needs to successfully compete with others. But this is the story of the poet's life, as I have said. And of course one must have a job that permits such time away.

➥ Keep a notebook. This is so obvious and so important that I may unconsciously say it many times in different ways throughout this book. "I repeat myself? Very well then, I repeat myself."

➥ Stay young. I don't mean the body—that's going to hell one way or another. I mean, when we first started to write we were a child sitting on the kitchen floor, playing with words. We must guard against ever getting too far from that child.

The Background Check

A low-rent, walk-up apartment building. When I knocked on the door a man wearing a T-shirt peered out over the safety chain. I told him my business and held up my private investigator ID. He opened the door. I walked in and heard the door close and lock behind us.

The place was a derangement of dirty clothes, stacks of old *LIFE* magazines, encrusted fast food containers, and guns. There were rifles and pistols mounted on most of the available wall space, and on a card table covered by a white towel in the middle of the room lay the pieces of what I guessed to be a dismantled machine gun. The room smelled of linseed oil and Chinese food.

When I looked at the man he was smiling at me, his hands in the pockets of paint-spattered black jeans, and I understood that he had been looking at me looking at the guns. His T-shirt was the sleeveless kind, and I took note of the well-developed shoulders, and the extreme whiteness of his arms—Wonder Bread white, almost the same color as his shirt.

"You're not a cop, are you?"

"No. Just a citizen."

"You sure?"

"Sure I'm sure—here, have another look at my ID."

He took it from me and studied the picture. He looked at me, then back at the photograph. He moved to the window and held the ID up to the sunlight. He casually plucked a German Luger from the wall and held it down by his side while he studied the picture in his other hand. He looked at me.

"I hate cops."

"They're no big pals of mine either."

"Is that right?" His eyebrows lifted in curious surprise.

"Absolutely. I never met one I liked."

"I'd kill a cop if he came into my house," he said, and flipped the ID like a baseball card to a spot on the floor halfway between our suddenly anchored bodies.

"Yeah, I would. Wouldn't be hard. Be easy. I wouldn't have no problem with that. If there was a cop here right now, in this room, I'd shoot him. Just like that, *pop*, easy. That's how much I hate cops."

I chuckled. "Well," I said, "I can appreciate that," and moved slowly to where my ID rested. And then, as I bent over to pick up the card, I talked. Fast and gentle, in a flood of speech, I agreed with him—how untrustworthy I'd found cops to be, how I ran into them a good deal in my line of work and never found them to be cooperative or pleasant or interested in anyone but themselves, how they lied and cheated and routinely took kickbacks and fucked off on the job and knew how to beat suspects so the beating wouldn't show, how they scarfed up evidential drugs and resold or used them themselves, and what, I went on, general all-around scum they were. How I was just a guy doing a job and could we perhaps talk about this man my client was thinking of hiring and needed a reference for, and I said the name, *Corey Jenkins*, which was real, though not the reason I gave for asking, and could you say something about the man, since I understood, my client understood, they had at one time been neighbors? Could you in good faith recommend him for a position of trust and responsibility? My voice pitched low and affable and off the cuff.

"Hey—no kidding, you know Corey?"

"Well, I don't know him. But my client's interested in hiring him for an important job."

"What job?"

"You know, they never tell me exactly what job. I'm just a peon, really. Just a working stiff, a messenger, kind of."

"Not a cop, eh?" He looked down at the Luger and covered the top of the chamber with his left hand . . . a calligraphy of grease in the lines across his knuckles. . . .

"No," I laughed. "No chance."

I kept a smile on but felt the right corner of my mouth twitching and turned my head slightly to give him just the left side. A cold bead of sweat streaked from my armpit and I clamped down on it. The man ambled closer to the window, still holding the Luger with two hands. He put one foot up on the radiator and looked out. He began to hum "Stardust," a wistful, or blank, expression on his face. It was difficult to tell from my angle. I considered talking again or edging my way toward the door, but at the moment it seemed best to be quiet and stay still. The man was relaxed; he had a light baritone voice and hummed on pitch. If he was also thinking of what was coming next I could not decipher his thoughts. He was just humming and looking out the window and holding a Luger.

"Mind if I smoke?" I asked, calm and low.

He wheeled suddenly toward me and said, in a loud voice, "Hey! Have a cancer stick! Who gives a fuck!"

I dropped my notebook and tried clumsily to catch it before it hit—the floors were bare hardwood, and the split-second idea was to avoid any dropping, striking, echoing noises of any kind. I was not fast enough of course and bent to pick the notebook up, praying at the same time that whatever was going to happen might happen quickly and without my conscious knowledge, and also reaching for smokes and lighter in my shirt pocket so that perhaps I might even have that cigarette, it was not too much to ask after all, was it, in the apocryphal last-wish stories, and besides it gave my hands something definite to do.

After I straightened up I did not look immediately at the man but lit a cigarette and inhaled deeply. My tie had gotten tossed up over my shoulder and I pulled it down and smoothed it with two fingers. The man was sitting on the radiator with his legs out and his hands on his knees, the gun matter-of-factly pinned under his right hand like a calm, lethal pet, a miniature Rottweiler made of metal.

"Shouldn't smoke," he said.

"I know, I know."

"Bad for you."

"Ain't it the truth."

"I quit, three weeks ago."

"Great! Good for you!"

He stood and walked slowly toward me, a rolling, affected gait, something picked up from the movies, the Luger swaying at the end of his arm like a weight tied to a rope. He stood close. Very dark brown eyes and black eyelashes, long and girlish. Large pores. His face smelling of soy sauce. He began to nod, very sagely, looking me flush in the eyes.

"He's all right."

"What?" I said, smiling insanely.

"Corey. Corey Jenkins. He's all right. He's righteous. He's okay."

I nodded along with him, stalling, trying to find a response.

"Oh!" I said finally. "Oh, right!" I uncapped my pen and scribbled something in my notebook. "Then you do know him?"

"Asshole buddies."

"That's terrific!" I said, nodding, backing away and moving toward the door. The man moved with me, matching my steps.

"That's just what I need. You've been a great help."

"That's it?"

"Yes, I think that's everything. You've been a great help— probably be responsible for getting Corey the job."

"What *is* the job?"

We were at the door. I had the knob in my hand.

"Don't know exactly, but one of trust and responsibility, you can be sure." I turned the knob both ways. Nothing. Again. He reached over my shoulder and threw the deadbolt.

"Thanks. Thanks a lot." I was in the hall, going down the stairs, backward, my hand on the wood banister.

"Hey—have a good day, all right? Later. Thanks for your help."

"Sure you're not a cop?"

"Ha ha—that's a good one! Take care!"

I was on the street, not running, but walking fast. If I turned and looked up I knew I would see him watching me from the fire escape and I had no heart for that. I walked one, two, five blocks without a single thought. Was I smoking, did I carry the notebook under my arm, did my tie fly up in the autumn breeze, in my haste? These are possible outcomes, like the possible paths of an electron. They must remain theoretical, since I cannot see them now, as I could not see them then.

Eventually, like the guy in the old joke, I turned into a luncheonette. I sat at the gray Formica counter and ordered coffee and a piece of coconut custard pie. I had no idea where my car was. My office did not know where I was. No one did. Way before cell phones and computers. More dangerous then, but easier to hide.

I was twenty-one years old, living with a dark-haired woman, my sights on two or three others. I had recently discovered poetry and found it almost as subversive as sex. What I had begun writing myself was bad, but I didn't know that and was proud of my bad poems and would keep trying, until one day I would write something real, a new creation, something that could walk and talk on its own. I would send it out into the world, and then keep trying for the rest of my life to repeat that act, and the feeling that accompanied it—a feeling somewhere between release from the body and having, for an instant, my young body, without a single impediment.

But I wasn't thinking of the future, or poetry. I wasn't thinking of anything. I was eating a slice of coconut custard pie.

The counterman was kind—he spread his hands and leaned toward me like a bartender and said "Everything okay?" as if he really wanted to know. The pie, I said, was *superb,* though I knew even as I said it that *superb* was wrong—wrong for a luncheonette in New Haven, wrong for the time of day, wrong for my age, my line of work.

But it was.

And everything I would need for eternity was suddenly present. Sunlight fell through the luncheonette window to the black and white octagonal floor tiles and blazed up, a clean light, and dust motes turned in that shaft like slow galaxies. I noticed the etched clarity of the salt shaker's crystal body, the noble humility of spoon and fork. I lifted the cup of coffee to my lips and breathed in the black, loamy smell. I cut the last bit of custard from its ruffled border and saw an exquisite pattern of air bubbles where the custard had cooled against the bottom crust.

I lifted it to my mouth.

I tell you, I nearly wept at the taste of that pie.

2. Finds the Liminal Place

The In-between • *Ignition* • *Let's Get Lost* •
A Pathway to the Gateway • *Meandering,*
Description, Music • *Not So Hot, Better, Limit*
Interference • *Top Ten Poet Complaints*

The smartest thing I ever did was to adopt a big, strong, beautiful cat. To write poetry, it helps to be in a liminal state. My cat has mastered this.

—Belle Waring

The In-between

Liminality: *Neither here nor there, the in-between, no man's land, a thin place, threshold between one state and another . . .*
   Can refer to:

Time—noon, midnight, dusk, solstice, equinox

Place—border, embassy, frontier, airport

Large-scale period—extended war, revolution, any period of flux, e.g., the American Civil Rights Movement

Transitional life stages—adolescence, dying

Neurological/psychological states—the moment of awakening from sleep (hypnopompic) or the moment of sliding into sleep (hypnagogic); drug states, hypnotic state, meditative state, danger-induced periods of hypersensory awareness, coma, the artistic mind during composition

Ignition

*Also, if possible, I like to clean the whole house before I start writing. I
rarely have time to do this, so sometimes I just wash the dishes.*
—Julia Story

It's early in the morning and I'm getting ready to write.

Breakfast has been eaten and coffee brewed. Now, it's as if
I'm a pilot entering the cockpit and going through the checklist in
preparation for a long flight.

I pour the first cup of coffee, carry it out onto the screened-
in sun porch and angle it on the side table, cup handle turned to
where my right hand will naturally fall. I adjust the cushions on the
rattan chair, then go upstairs and bring down a kid's tiny rocker with
matching pillow to use as footrest.

I open the cold doors of the cast-iron stove and sweep last night's
ashes out and into a metal bucket. Since it's been raining for days the
wood stored outside is damp and impossible to ignite without help,
so I place a fire starter made of compressed wood and kerosene on
the grate and light each end.

Silence, I once thought, was necessary. At least I preferred it.
But lately I've come to use instrumental music as writing's aural
background. Different types of writing seem to require different
music. This period of writing's accompaniment has been a
postclassical album by Max Richter called *Songs from Before,* played
over and over. It's not yet emptied out its interest and I'll stay with
it until it does. I wriggle in my earphones, switch to iPod on my
phone, and cue Richter up.

I've taken myself away to a rustic cabin on the far shore of Green
Bay, Wisconsin, for two weeks. That sounds like I'm roughing it in
semiwilderness, on my own. But no. Sarah is here too. And civilization's right down the road, where the town's year-round population
of 358 swells to several thousand in the summer. Still, cell phone
reception is spotty to nonexistent, and this is a relief.

The water's flat gray, the same shade upwards to sky, with green interruptions for the jut of Peninsula Park and, a bit farther over on the horizon, Horseshoe Island. This means I have no meteorological reasons not to write, the temptations of sun and swimming having been removed from my book of excuses and procrastinations.

And: *I'm happy.*

No other occupation, no task or activity I've done has used as much of myself—whatever *self* might mean—as writing a poem. In fact, in the heat of a new poem it often feels like I'm using more of me than there *is*. Far-flung facts, memories, intuitions, snatches of song, metaphors, and a host of other felicities I didn't know I knew, come spinning toward me on the fly, as if by magnetic attraction. Or, to put it romantically, I'm sometimes joined in the writing by an angel who goes by my name, but writes with divine wisdom and joy.

The pleasure is not unalloyed, of course: writing is a combination of intense and sustained excitement, *and* anxiety of the most base and existential sort. One only hopes for two things: first, to begin. And then: to find that flow, that angelic rift of song so irresistible one *must* follow, and anxiety is rendered moot, and disappears.

The coffee is on a short side table to my right. I sip a little, then take a substantial slug. The earthy black heat fills my mouth, then radiates down through the rest of my body. I bless the first human to pluck a coffee bean, and the one who figured out how to roast and brew it. Coffee pulls the trigger.

On another table to my right is a stack of books. Many are volumes of poetry I've been saving all year, holding myself back from opening until this very moment. I will dip in and out during the writing. I've also stockpiled science books—popular physics and neurobiology for the layman—which light up some rarely used part of the brain, a part I'd like to invite to the party. Lastly, a few current issues of *National Enquirer* and *Globe*, which I use as writing rest stops, as brain candy. And, to be frank, I *like* the vulgar energy of gossip. It reminds me of my peasant roots.

The fire has taken off now, and will not need feeding or poking for a while. I open my leather portfolio, with its yellow legal pad and three pens, one a vintage fountain pen with flexible nib and smooth ink flow, the other two extra-fine-point roller balls. Richter's music, with its intentional background of static and low indiscernible speaking voices, begins. I look out the window at dark-edged scallops moving across the water like cursive sentences, then at the tarnished clouds above, the tree leaves that reach out over the water and shake gently in morning wind. And, as they did when I was a kid in a classroom and it was forbidden to look out the window, my eyes unfocus, my mind loosens and drifts. Far off, I hear the blood begin to hum.

This was always the journey I desired.

Let's Get Lost

. . . a life of writing books is a trying adventure in which you cannot find out where you are unless you lose your way.

—Philip Roth (*The Counterlife*)

There are hundreds of versions of the Hansel and Gretel story. European, African, Russian, and Latin versions of the tale have been collected. The notion that in times of scarcity abandoning offspring might be a reasonable option is apparently widespread.

POLICE: COUPLE TRIED TO SELL BABY AT WALMART

Associated Press Jun 25th 2010 10:28AM
SALINAS, Calif. (AP) – A California couple faces child endangerment charges after police say they tried to sell their 6-month-old baby for $25 outside a Walmart store.

It's generally a brother and sister, left to fend for themselves in a forest. In spite of the fact that their situation is dire, as they wander they share their small store of food with various birds and animals along the way. Eventually they encounter a witch who lives in a tasty cottage and seems to have the children's best interests at heart.

But, as so often happens, what at first appears to be altruism turns out to be grotesque self-interest: the witch has cannibalistic designs. Each child is kept in a cage and fattened up like a Christmas goose. It is a terrifying situation.

From our psychologized, child-centered age we may righteously wonder, *What could the cruel parents who told their kids* this *story possibly have been thinking?* The versions of such folktales gathered by the Brothers Grimm (could there be more aptly named ethnographers?) are unacceptable in contemporary American life. Disney began scrubbing them up in the forties, though their versions do retain at least some of the terror. More current iterations are so anemic as to be unrecognizable.

33

Of course, middle-school kids know how to instantly find videos of actual beheadings. Stripped of moral context, today's daily outrages barely register. Strangely, the Grimm stories both supersede and *contain* such contemporary horrors, in terms of psychological accuracy, resonance, and subversion.

We swim in irony.

Hansel and Gretel eventually outwit the witch and find their way back home, for when innocence is joined with kindness (sharing food with the weak) it is rewarded.

The children are usually reunited with the parents, and in most versions do not extract vengeance for their abandonment. At least, not on the repentant father. The stepmother is another story (biological mom is often missing from the start; death from childbirth?). Poor stepmother: a universally despised figure. She always has to go. And the end for her is always particularly nasty.

But, really, how good is a father who can be convinced to desert his own children? The father always seemed to me more culpable than the witch. The witch is only following her nature—she was born to eat children. But to intentionally ditch two kids in a creepy forest . . .

Life must have been exceedingly brutal, and not, Dear Reader, too long ago. Every time I read a Grimm story I realize how much I *like* civilization, with its rule of law, its air conditioning, its room service.

The only thing worse than a child-eating witch would be one of those *real* monsters who rape and kill children.

Part of the story is saying: if an evil can be imagined by humans, it will eventually break through to reality. It *will* happen.

Some things have improved. Just—not us.

What does all this have to do with poetry and writing?

Thank you for asking.

It's dangerous getting lost. Even the kind of psychic and psychological lostness that's part of every moderately successful poet's story involves danger. And yet the writer must. What do I mean by getting lost in this way?

I think it goes hand in hand with a passionate and irrational commitment to poetry. You *do* have to enter a forest, again and again. It may be an especially beautiful forest, but there's no guarantee that you will find your way home again, or bring anything back with you if you do. You have to enter the forest at the beginning, and you have to reenter it at various times later on. There is, as far as I can see, no retirement. In addition to these lost episodes in the larger, metaphorical forest, you have to get more immediately and literally lost *every single time* you face the white page and the words begin to appear (or don't) and you follow, with no idea where you'll end up.

It isn't hard to enter. Students come to me all the time and lay their love of poetry on the table. They are passionate and open-hearted. Poetry jazzes them, like nothing else. They can't get enough. They want to be a poet more than anything in the world. Their skin is smooth; the whites of their eyes, clear. They sit facing me, perched on the edge of a steel and plastic, university-provided chair, fresh-born poem in hand, vibrating. *Nothing* has ever gotten to them like this poetry thing—not music, not money, not love.

And then sometime later they drop by my office again to say casually they are applying to law school, just as, you know, a backup. Okay, fine. I would not tell anyone to throw a life away on such an unprofitable venture as poetry.

But hedging your bet won't work. When you get lost in poetry you don't get to take a GPS. I don't say you have to eat/sleep/think poetry every moment of your life (though it wouldn't hurt, at least not in the beginning). I mean all thoughts of safety, of following some prescribed path, of making a lot of money, of pleasing your parents and/or your spouse—you gotta give up. And not just once and for all. No, *every time* you face the blank page, all down a dim unscannable future, you will have to get lost. Even after the prize, or when you get the coveted fellowship, or snag the two-course-load position, publish the book. To begin the next book, the next poem, you will have to wander freshly.

Nothing in life is certain; it's less certain as a poet. You have to commit to the uncertainty. You have to commit to unreasonable devotion, and to an art that, though practiced by many, is appreciated by very few. Even the word for what you try to do, *poetry*, can't be defined. Not really.

You have to get lost. And you don't even get a sack of bread-crumbs to lay down for the journey back.

A Pathway to the Gateway

I am an intensely physical person, and completely distractible. It is difficult
for me to stop moving, thinking, doing. The longer I am a writer, the more I
understand that my monkey mind must be tricked into stillness.

—Ann Townsend

Poet alertness makes for a busy brain. But then so does schizophrenia. Let's face it: being alive in twenty-first-century America makes for a busy brain.

Poets, with their already hyperactive sensibility, need a filter. Some sort of calm is required for writing poems (*recollection in tranquility*), though the activity itself can be done in the midst of chaos. Every writer with a child has to learn this, or stop writing. Or give the child up for adoption. Many have been tempted.

How to slow the barrage of information and stimulation surrounding us . . .

And then there's the purely practical outer problem: how to find time and psychic space to write, while at the same time making a living and having some sort of life that includes others.

For the writer in particular, balance between the poles of activity and calm is a consuming and continuing question.

The moderately successful poet finds ways and means to limit the incoming signal. This is an increasingly difficult task. I won't reiterate the incursion of modern media on contemporary sensibility—Internet, Twitter, chat—everyone knows.

But it was, in a sense, ever so. Rilke left the messy responsibilities of wife and child and somehow charmed his way into the windswept battlements of castles owned by rich women. *Then* he could write, "And who, if I cried out, would hear me among the angelic orders?"

W. H. Auden, when teaching at Bennington, ate cold cereal in the school cafeteria at every meal. When people on a train or plane asked him what he did for a living he would say, Medieval Historian.

That stopped conversation cold, sure enough. He pissed in the sink, he drank like a fish. Auden knew how to limit stimulus input.

Some writers have found that wearing the same clothes every day frees up a helpful byte or two of concentration. The solution for others may be opposite: John Cheever dressed in suit and tie, got on a commuter train and wrote every day in his "office"—a small janitor's closet in Manhattan.

Speaking of Auden and Cheever, many writers and poets have noticed the nerve-steadying (at least at first) powers of booze and some drugs. Alcoholics often have what has been called "hyper-augmentation," a medical way of saying they are more sensitive than average to outside stimuli—noises are louder, colors brighter, etc. Sometimes I think artists also must have this dubious gift.

Alcohol tamps down an overactive sensibility. And it has the added benefit (?) of amplifying fantasy and grandiosity. This theory at least goes some way toward explaining why at least five of eleven American Nobel Prize winners in Literature died alcoholic deaths.

Healthier, longer-lasting poets find modes of personal discipline that limit the incoming signals, and allow some measure of calm even in the midst of a busy life. The hard-drinking, womanizing, physically inert model of the roaring poet invented by poor Dylan Thomas on his whirlwind American reading tours and since imitated by many is long dead and gone. Today's poets are much more likely to do regular workouts, drink socially (or at least plan binges to avoid professional embarrassment) and take their hard-earned academic posts so seriously that any hanky-panky or "systematic derangement of the senses" is viewed more as threat to tenure than bohemian poetic license.

I suppose the very best thing a poet can do is to be born rich, with genes wired for long life. If you can't manage both money and genes, go for the long genes. If you've been blessed with neither, marry a doctor and write fast.

Meandering, Description, Music

Get off the subject.
—Richard Hugo

We often enter the liminal when we slip off the point. I'm not speaking of those people who, in conversation, begin a statement or story with the beginning of a sentence, then immediately interrupt that sentence with some qualification and/or extraneous detail, which leads them down still another digressive trail, and so on, until both of you have forgotten what the whole peroration was supposed to be about in the first place, and you realize this person will *never* get to the end of his/her sentence, and you begin wishing for a nearby explosion, or The Rapture, or some other major event that would abruptly end both your sufferings, and relieve you of the mounting urge to reach out and strangle him/her with your bare hands. This is not the type of digression I recommend.

But poetry, it seems, *is* what's going on in the corner of our eyes (mind) when we're looking straight ahead and concentrating on Important Matters. In fact, it would be much better when we sit down (or stand, or lie) to write poetry if we just banish *the idea* of poetry, and *the hope* for poetry, from our heads. Better if we just fill a page with words. Pretend we're writing marginalia, rather than the body of the text. Meander. Meandering can connect us with that wider, wilder stream of imagery and language that flows just beneath bright-light consciousness.

I want to encourage you to trust this impulse, the impulse to meander or digress—follow it, let it take you away from the point. Hang in there and see how long the impulse lasts, and if it will branch off into still other digressions. Let it carry you, like the current of a river, where it wants. Don't struggle. You won't drown. Remember, the worst that can happen is that what ends up on the page is crap. And all writers must get used to *that* dirt-common eventuality. And what do you do if that is the result of your meandering? You ball up the paper and throw it in the can. You go out for ice cream, and the next morning suit up and show up, try it all over again.

But ah, what *may* happen! You may be led as if by accident to a voice you didn't know lived in you, and to images, statements, remembrances, syntactical moves—all raw and shocking as just-opened oysters. Things never dreamed of in your philosophy, Horatio.

I am suggesting nothing new, of course. What I speak of goes by many names—*free writing, writing off the subject, stream of consciousness, automatic writing, subconscious writing,* etc. If you Google these terms you'll find some interesting history, as well as many concrete instructions on *how* one free-writes, inter alia.

What I have been suggesting in this chapter—*getting lost, creative meandering*—are other ways of thinking about the same process. They are my metaphorical gateways to the liminal. There are a thousand ways to put these gateways into practice, and there are many eccentric methods that are one of a kind—Schiller's rotten apples, Proust's madeleine. . . . I have, earlier in this chapter, tried to be more specific about *things one can do* to enter the liminal. You will, if you persist, through trial and error find your own specific drawer of rotten apples, your madeleine. I want to talk now about one such method that is straightforward and has worked over and over for many poets.

I don't know how it is in music composition, but in writing I have found that it's best to just begin writing—putting words on the page. Then, trust, trust and follow.

Doing leads to discovery; *thinking* about doing rarely does.

Sometimes however the difficult part is *beginning.* There is often an opaque ganglion of nerves between the pen and the first word on the page. The invaluable American poet Charles Wright has said he typically begins a poem by looking at the sky and the physical world around him, and then lets what he sees enter words. I too work this way. Many times before I have finished a description (and I imagine this may be so for Wright, too) something totally unrelated starts to enter the stream of language and I am off, meandering.

But if that does not happen, at least I have a description of something. Which may be valuable on its own. I may use it then, or later (save everything!) as seed for a more complete treatment. It may be gateway not only to the liminal but also to first contact between the poem and its readers.

Beginning with the visible has that advantage—it is, generally speaking, part of our shared reality. And the implications inherent in such poems often reach beyond the moment as well as beyond the material, what we think of as concrete reality. One need only look, for example, at the "thing" poems of French poet Francis Ponge to see how "simple" description may lead to profound delight, to milestones of happy collision between language and the material world.

It is all a way to catch hold of the music of language. When I asked poet Michael Dickman if he could share with me any habits that he had found helpful in writing poems he wrote back: "My habit of mind is that there is something I want to hear that I can't quite hear. But almost, almost."

The music of poetry is always there. But just out of reach. I like that notion; it seems exactly right. We look for ways to come closer to the sound, or ways to go to where the sound is clearer and louder, and sometimes we succeed. Some of us develop complex rituals or superstitions. Some of these work some of the time; none are failsafe. Many or most poets will say that they hardly ever think about inspiration or the muse, because it gets them nowhere, and they have to write regularly, with or without inspiration.

But there is always an element of either chance or grace involved in writing poetry; I don't believe the muse is total fantasy. It is a matter, as in much of life, of finding what we can control and what we cannot. And then concentrating our efforts on what is within our control, and letting go of the rest. There *are* methods that may bring us to the liminal state, methods that have been tested and proven by poets past and present. But even in the liminal state we can't be sure that what we hear is the real deal, or some form of interesting nonsense. Listen, listen: you can move yourself closer to the angel, but you can't make her sit down and whisper in your ear.

This is why, I think, Eliot said, "Only humility is endless."

Not So Hot, Better, Limit Interference

Here are some concrete means, outside the accident of lucky DNA, that moderately successful poets have done/are doing to find the gateway to the liminal, as well as a few cautions:

Not So Hot Methods:

➡ Drink & drug.

➡ Stay in bed all day (*pace* John & Yoko).

➡ Follow any guru *too* closely.

➡ Join a monastery (there are examples of this working—there's lots of in-between in monasteries—but generally your *liminal* time goes to God, not the muse).

➡ Live a continuously dramatic life (affairs, betrayals, and weasel behavior of all kinds—e.g., politics—and so on).

➡ Disregard those closest to you (well, this actually works for some—try it, if you don't mind being a schmuck for life).

Better:

➡ Learn another language, a musical instrument, or a trade involving physical skills (may not get you to the liminal right away, but the process of study of such disciplines—ones involving both physical and cognitive dimensions—tend to bring the liminal up close and personal).

➡ Meditate.

➡ Nap (see above).

➡ Spend time by large bodies of water, or mountains, or forests.

➡ Listen to music that's new to you. Listen to music you loved long ago.

➡ Read. Read. Read.

➡ When grief comes, give in to it utterly.

Limit Interference:

➡ Know when to say no. *Say* no.

➡ Develop a fair idea of what your time is worth in \$\$, and ask for a little more.

➡ Procrastinate wisely.

➡ Learn to recognize fools approaching. If cornered, do not suffer them long, or at all.

➡ Put family in a privileged place, but not in the way of poetry.

➡ Use all electronics as rarely as possible, and as tools only (TV may serve as useful sedative).

➡ Face time, *yea*; social media, *nay*.

TOP TEN POET COMPLAINTS

10. Learn at last moment that reading you've been invited to give at local community college happens *after* open mike.

9. Wikipedia keeps removing my bio.

8. My novel, about a poet in a crappy relationship, whose book of poems keeps being chosen as contest finalist, has been turned down more times than my latest book of poems.

7. Guy I went to school with has yet *another* poem in *The New Yorker*.

6. AWP keeps turning down my panel on (YOUR NAME HERE): *Neglected Original, Neglected Master*.

5. I haven't heard of a *single* person in this lit mag.

4. So, I guess you have to be *famous* to be in this lit mag.

3. Submitted book to contest, did not win contest, publisher keeps sending me fundraising letters beginning "Dear Friend of Poetry."

2. Billy Collins.

1. Why couldn't it be *me*? Why, why not *me*?

3. MAKES USE

Phil, & Company • *Crafty Craft* •
O, Research • *The Private I* • *Bobby the Ape* •
Top Ten Questions Poets Are Always Asked

Make use of the things around you . . .
Put it all in,
Make use.
　　　　　　　—Ray Carver, "Sunday Night"

Phil, & Company

Phil Levine told our class at Columbia we were too impatient—
we wanted to sing before we could speak. Lots of students were
handing in poems that *sounded* slick and smart but did not hold
up under clear-eyed, bullshit-detecting scrutiny, which Phil was
most happy to provide. Other students wrote versions of the
then current mode—sincere, lyric-narrative poems that reliably
contained, like the prize in a box of Cracker Jacks, an epiphany.

On the first day of our workshop Phil asked, "Are there any
geniuses in this room?" No one raised a hand or said a word.
"Good," Phil said. "I have nothing to teach a genius, and a genius
sure doesn't need this class. Also, I am not a genius. If I were I
wouldn't be teaching. I'd be writing genius poems. Now that *that's*
out of the way, we can get to work."

Tess Gallagher was all the rage, and in the middle of another
day of workshop Phil was obviously exasperated by the prospect
of discussing yet another Gallagher knockoff, one that we had
just begun to workshop. He suddenly struck the table with his
knuckles, a light knock, and pushed the poem away toward the
center of the conference table. He closed his eyes, and then just
sat, doing nothing. The author of the abandoned poem stared at
Phil, her expression an anxious mix of terror and hope beyond
hope. The rest of us held our collective breath, not knowing what
the hell to expect.

"Tess is *fine*," Phil said finally, "but if you're gonna steal, go
back and steal from the old guys—go to Keats, go to Hardy. Find
out why they're still around. See what you can do with that."

Then he took Hardy's "Transformations" from his notebook
and read it to us. Twice. Here's the poem:

Transformations

Portion of this yew
Is a man my grandsire knew,
Bosomed here at its foot:
This branch may be his wife,
A ruddy human life
Now turned to a green shoot.

These grasses must be made
Of her who often prayed,
Last century, for repose;
And the fair girl long ago
Whom I often tried to know
May be entering this rose.

So, they are not underground,
But as nerves and veins abound
In the growths of upper air,
And they feel the sun and rain,
And the energy again
That made them what they were!

He let that sink in. In the silence, Phil was teaching.

Then he picked up the poor woman's workshop poem and launched into the devastation.

The main sources of nourishment and inspiration for an apprentice poet are:

➡ *Teachers;*

➡ *Other poems, current and past;*

➡ *Individual experience—cognitive, sensory, and emotional.*

In other words:

Digesting other poems + Teacher example + Alertness to sensory/cognitive data = Growth as poet.

Sometimes there is confluence between these sources. Often, the poet experiences them as competing. This tension is the heart of the poet's apprenticeship.

Love of poems by others x Resistance to influence = Style

Although these equations and others must be solved by the student alone, the journey can be considerably streamlined and assisted by a poet who has already done the math, and emerged on the other side intact: a teacher.

Where does one find a teacher of poetry? Once, young writers gathered informally, and those with more experience served as teachers. They passed their work around, talked endlessly about influences, and taught each other—Paris in the twenties is one famous example. New York City in the 1930s–60s is another. But now every major world city that might have served as similar meeting place for young artists and writers is forbiddingly expensive. Older writers, poets in particular, who once would have congregated in urban centers are now spread out across the country. Many teach in colleges and universities. Others work at jobs in editing, publishing, advertising, or business.

The place they come together today, and where students may find the teachers meant for them, is the MFA program. I don't see this fact as lamentable, though like every writer I know I would have loved to have rubbed elbows with the modernists in Twenties Paris. No, it's just the way things are. And, there *are* advantages.

It's easy to satirize writing workshops, and MFA programs in general. Pomposity tends to cluster around people engaged in ambitious work, particularly artistic work, which attempts to combine rigor and mystery.

But workshops, in spite of their inadequacies, provide beginning poets with a megadose of at least half of the above equations. The older poet recommends poets and poems based on what the student's discernible *individual* needs are—what poets may be necessary to excite/provoke that student at that moment, in just the way needed to move the student to the next level of practice.

The poet/teacher also, of course, looks at the *student's* poems— through the lens of thousands of hours of devoted reading in the fields of poetry and elsewhere, as well as uncounted time spent laboring on her/his own poems. What the poet/teacher then gives the student in "feedback" is itself a minor artistic product—pitched in tone and content to, again, *provoke* either growth or fruitful rebellion in the student. It just happens that in this case the audience for the result is one.

Additionally the MFA experience itself, the whole package, tells students, by surrounding them with peers and teachers and even an institutional edifice all devoted in a nearly sacramental way to writing, that this odd preoccupation with the making of poems is a *valuable, useful* way to spend two years, or maybe much more. It tells students that they are not crazy for thinking a life in poetry, in twenty-first-century America, is a life well spent.

But in addition to these benefits, tangible and intangible, an MFA program offers one other major advantage difficult to obtain outside such programs: it allows students to study, close up and in the flesh, practicing poets—their teachers. It lets students see what such a life looks like, the life of a man or woman who has already achieved the desired, though culturally indeterminate, status of moderately successful poet. It gives the student living models—concrete ways of being—to either emulate or reject. And this, in the end, may be *the most* important part of any poet's apprenticeship.

Back to that first workshop with Phil Levine. Phil was my hero, my favorite poet. I would ask him to direct my thesis. He would love and praise my work. We would become friends.

This was my fantasy. And in fact, my first workshop with Philip Levine did arrive, though it had seemed to me extraordinarily long in coming, long as a kid's Christmas Eve, or any coming event the imagination has multiplied by desire.

Mirabilis!—Phil shuffled through the pile of poems in front of him and pulled out *my very own!* But instead of asking me to read it, and then soliciting student response—which was the convention of all previous workshops I'd been in—he immediately read my poem out loud, in his nasal voice, accompanied by a barely discernable though still alarming edge of sarcasm. At least, that's what I heard. Probably just my nerves, I thought to myself. I hoped no one else had heard it.

Phil finished reading and paused briefly. I looked furtively around the table.

And then without ceremony he proceeded to eviscerate my poem. He tore it a new one. He said it was *crap, a "B movie" poem.* Sometimes we were in the mood for a B movie, he granted, and B movies could be entertaining in their way, in a trivial way. Then he went on to talk about some of his favorite B movies, most from the thirties and forties. He ridiculed them, but also paid them homage, at least for taking people's minds off darker matters.

But that was the problem. Poems should contain those darker matters that B movies skirted. Sure, such faux art did satisfy some of our baser fantasies and desires. But that didn't change the fact that they were . . . crap. Like my poem. My poem was crap.

Any comments?

There were none. I think we must have gone on to discuss the other workshop poems after that, but I have no recollection. I was in a blackout. The next thing I remember is walking out of the classroom, and several of my fellow student poets gently patting my back and saying things like, "Don't worry, man—I hear he does that to every first poem in a workshop," and, "Oh, Jeff, are you all right?"

I hurried from the building after class and went directly to the West End Café. I drank a beer and three shots of Seagram's Seven as quickly as I could, then left before any of my classmates could arrive for the traditional post-workshop cocktail hour debriefing. I could not bear to suffer any further consolation.

What rose in me in the days and weeks after this class was not resignation or despair but *anger*, anger and defiance. *No way this is the end of it, Levine,* I said to the man in my mind. *I'm going to write other poems—much better poems—and you are going to like them, you are going to like my poems and you are going to like me. Yes, and you will direct my thesis, too.* I had many conversations with the poet god Philip Levine, who had destroyed me, though no one but me was privy to them. I could not wait to prove him wrong, to make him see how wrong he was. I seethed, and planned, and wrote.

My reaction could have been otherwise. I had seen students whose confidence was destroyed by comments received in workshop. A few had simply dropped out. I was once standing in the hall talking to a fellow student at Columbia when a woman burst from Phil's office, sobbing. I found out later that day that Phil had turned down her thesis; she would not get her degree.

Others continued after taking critical beatings, but clearly made some inner adjustments. Their comments in workshop afterward became reflexively qualified, their general manner a kind of meek hesitation. Their expectations as to what the rest of their degree might give them, and what they themselves might have to add to poetry, were severely diminished.

Teachers have power.

I don't know why I didn't react this way. I have come to believe that in addition to talent a kind of stubbornness is also necessary for life as a poet. Or maybe it's defiance. Or maybe both qualities are wrapped up in *toughness*. Whatever one calls it, the result is a refusal to believe it when the world or some part of the world tells you that what you've made is no damn good, and implies (or says bluntly) that you should *not quit your day job.* The urge or desire to prove oneself, to redouble effort and resolve when faced with rejection, is essential. I had this refusal—it rose up in me without summons—and used it to good purpose with Levine. But it was hardly the only or the last time in my life I've made use of it. *Ars longa, vita brevis* . . . for the artist, the power to reject rejection is the gift that keeps giving.

Phil and my other teachers taught me many things. They taught me to read a poem like a poet, and the difference between that and reading for pleasure. Some of the writers they introduced me to became seminal to my own poetry. They spoke candidly about their own practice, and that generosity gave me methods of composition to emulate, or react against. They taught me what was important about a line, a musical phrase, a stanza. They taught me to recognize convention and dead language, especially in that place where it is hardest for all writers to discern—my own poems. I learned that writing poetry, especially writing poetry after the age of thirty or forty, depends more on character than talent or luck.

I made use of my teachers. And I hope they made use of me. As a teacher myself I've found that the articulation of aesthetic choices for students forces me to continually examine and refresh those choices in my own work. They keep coming, these students of poetry, and I'm grateful for that. Their enthusiasm and desire lets me know that I've dedicated my life to a worthwhile cause. At this point I don't think I need that confirmation to keep writing, but I am grateful for it. Yes—I can use it.

I think Phil saw what reared up in me thirty years ago at Columbia. I think he recognized my reaction and respected it. He knew his way of teaching made use of strong challenge, and he had seen students react to it differently. He'd been teaching long enough to see what worked—who survived and who didn't.

In any case I did begin to write better poems in that semester (though not many, really). Phil began to say good things about them, and I asked him to direct my thesis. Before he agreed he asked how old I was. When I told him—twenty-eight—he nodded and said, approvingly, "You're a grown-up man."

During our meetings about the thesis I remember very little discussion of the actual poems—"These you should take out; the others are fine," was what I remember as the extent of Phil's counsel in that arena. What we talked about was my life—my job, my wife, where I'd come from, what my parents were like, sports I played, books I read, movies I loved. Phil would ask questions about these things as if he really was interested, and after I'd answered he'd respond with answering moments or situations from his life. I began to think that Phil really *was* interested in me, in my life.

"You're a grown-up man." I see now that he meant this as both compliment and challenge. There were other simple, but affirming comments like this every time I saw him, at Columbia, and in all the years since. When I looked at Phil, at his way of being in the world— the way he did not suffer fools, his combination of rigor and gruff humor, his surprising sweetness—I saw a way through my own life. It wasn't that I wanted to *be* Phil; it was that Phil said by example that I could be what I was, *had* to be what I was, in fact; and that would be enough.

Phil knew he wasn't a genius; he was no Keats, the poet he especially loved. He knew without illusion that he was stuck with himself, and he had long ago found a way to go beyond acceptance of that fact, to take acceptance of limitation all the way to delight. Phil got pissed off about things, sure. But he took the world as it was, and he loved what he had.

Yes, that was what I wanted to get to.

I had three other workshop teachers at Columbia: Dan Halpern, Howard Moss, and David Ignatow.

Dan had a large Art Garfunkel Afro, and smoked a pipe. He was affable, and nice to me in a distant, bemused way—I was not much younger than him. I felt he was mostly interested in women students, and in his own career.

And why not? Dan was single, a successful poet and publisher, and teaching at Columbia. He had created *Antaeus*, then the hottest literary magazine on the planet. He'd published several books of his own poetry with a major press. Why would he not try and cash in on what Freud called the rewards of artistic success: money, fame, beautiful lovers.

Once when I had an appointment with him he was late and, sitting there in his office waiting I could not control my curiosity and got up to look at the stuff on his desk. Amid the pipe paraphernalia and piles of papers, files, and books there was a notepad with a hasty, barely legible scribble, *Pulitzer* it said—*Strand, Kinnell,* me?

The only thing I remember from his class was that Dan made us write a poem in syllabics, which I found interesting. I liked the resource of form in general; sonnets, sestinas, villanelles. They provided a kind of grid for my chaotic, twenty-something emotions. And they gave me a firmer sense of accomplishment when I finished than most of my free-verse attempts; after all, I had made a verbal object that satisfied certain difficult formal requirements, the same ones that poets like Shakespeare and Keats and Eliot and so many other legendary figures had submitted themselves to before me. Working in received forms connected me with an unbroken lineage of poets, the greats and near-greats as well as the forgotten. I was a craftsman. And the pride of craft is no small thing.

But back to Dan, who was a man of few words, content to let students handle the workshop discussion of poems. When a student graduated and plunged into the vast pool of applicants for a tiny number of university creative writing jobs, Dan's letters of recommendation were vague as pipe smoke, and around three sentences long.

Mostly I remember him sitting at the head of the long workshop table in Dodge Hall, aloof from the discussion unwinding before him, the white fluorescent air of the room vibrating with barely concealed aggression and envy, and Dan serenely puffing on his pipe, smoke engulfing and drifting through the denser cloud of his Afro, so that he appeared to be, not a man with his head in the clouds, but a man with a head made of clouds.

I admired Dan's understated version of ambition for poetry, for women. For me, at that time, they often seemed the same ambition.

———

I looked forward to David Ignatow's class, since I loved his poems, many of which were compressed, minimalist but searing accounts of working in his father's business. At the time I was working in *my* father's business, and I was sure that we would have much in common. I admired the brutal honesty of his books, as well as the way they combined a kind of "office and factory realism" with surreal, dream images.

But by the time I got to him Ignatow seemed tired of teaching, and/or tired of students. Maybe he was just tired. Maybe it was me and my poems, and not any others, that evoked his boredom. My poems of that time certainly would've bored me, the me of now. In any case, his response to my poems was perfunctory.

And response is what a student in a writing workshop wants most of all: the secret wish for voluminous (and mostly *positive*) feedback, on *my poems*, by the teacher.

Ignatow was not interested in finding out what, if anything, he and I had in common. I can remember nothing of what was said on either side in our conferences. I don't think Ignatow ever looked me in the eye. I barely registered for him, and my memory of the semester is a disappointment muffled by shadow.

He spooked me. Even though he had published his poems everywhere, and was as famous as a poet could be, he seemed embittered, sour, a man incapable of real pleasure. Again, this may be unfair. But I can't help or change my own very possibly distorted impressions. I can only admit that in those days, probably because I had only an inkling of who *I* was supposed to be, my view of others was often skewed.

But even mistaken impressions may be instructive: what I saw in Ignatow showed me a way I *didn't* want to be. He was like my personal Ghost of Poetry Future: without saying much of anything, Ignatow said *Jeff, leave your father's business. Don't stay past all hope of later joy.*

———

58

Howard Moss was a different story. He was short and balding, and his round glasses and hooded eyes made him look like a sleepy owl. Unlike almost all the other teachers at Columbia, Howard *dressed* for class—suit, or sportcoat and tie, usually a bowtie, and shined, laced-up shoes. He was immaculate in all areas of behavior and taste, including poetry, and he favored the finely made, the polished. But he also praised and welcomed a restrained wildness just below the surface of the words; this was most apparent in his devotion to the work of his contemporary, Elizabeth Bishop.

At the time Bishop was publishing almost all her poems in *The New Yorker*. Howard often brought a poem of Bishop's to class, ostensibly for discussion, but I think really to show us what the best poetry of the moment looked and felt like. I think he was actually a little in love with Elizabeth. In any case she was the perfect *New Yorker* poet, and he was the perfect poetry editor for *The New Yorker*.

After class Howard and I would often take the same downtown subway. We got along well, recognizing in each other a shared sense of dry, absurdist humor. We'd sit or stand through the subway ride, bantering about the workshop, or other poet teachers at Columbia, or poets at large, generally the ones who were hot at the moment. Howard never said anything cruel; cruelty wasn't in him. But he could and did dismantle pretension, artistic and personal, with a few hilarious, deadpan barbs. The only area Howard's humor could not penetrate was his own hypochondria. He had it bad. If the conversation turned to his latest cold or other affliction I learned quickly to respond with sympathetic gravity, then change the subject.

I wish I could tell you some of what we actually said. But who can remember, really, casual subway conversations covered over by thirty years of births and deaths, jobs, publications, honors, rejections, different gigs in different states, various loves and dismissals? I *could* imagine and reconstruct (I do remember Howard saying of my then hero, W. S. Merwin, that he was the most beautiful man he'd ever seen in real life; it struck me at the moment that Merwin had maybe *too* much going for one guy), but I hate when people do that and pretend it's what people actually said, word for word, and that somehow they remember. Besides, other people (Dana Gioia comes to mind) knew Howard better than I, and have written well about him.

Simply put, I liked Howard and he liked me, and the affection we shared was a small, non-earthshaking thing. It's cheering to think that the quiet attachments from that era are the ones that stay with me. I can go back now to a brisk fall, to walking up from Riverside on 116th Street, shooing pigeons from Grant's tomb as I hurry past, on my way to workshop after eating a sandwich on a bench by the river. I can see my teacher's owlish face in the jostle and blinking glare of the subway car after class; I remember the feeling of gratitude and affection, the love of student for teacher.

I like the fact that even writing this much has brought back some of that time and those teachers. It's all right that writing is inexact at best, a kind of lie. I like what is possible for me to write and how it points, in its clumsy way, to what can't be said, to what is lost. It is enough.

Crafty Craft

Some products of what we commonly think of as "craft"—Japanese baskets, cabinetry, letterpress books, to name just a few—occasionally achieve such levels that they leap into the category of "art." Filmmaking, I would say, is also a craft that sometimes produces art. I love movies, and I have seen thousands in my lifetime. But very few handmade baskets, and very few movies, deserve to be called "art."

I know: thousands of *poems* are published each year and few of those deserve the designation of art. A very good point. But even an "average," good old B movie can be just what one needs for an escape from the pressures of contemporary life, and an unbeautiful basket can still carry things.

But what is the possible use of a bad, or even average, poem? What, in fact, does that mean—"average poem"?

Something different is going on with poems, those strange verbal objects that even to poets often seem purposeless, nonutilitarian word clouds—floating around in a larger, bustling, more solid world.

We think the story of craft is simpler, that of course we know what craft is, but I would like to suggest here that the complexity of its relation to poetry blurs our notions of both.

I'd like to further suggest that even as we accept the mystery of art, we also accept the mystery of craft, at least when it comes to poetry.

I no longer believe that there is any one aspect of writing poems—how to break lines, for example—which is detachable from all other aspects. One cannot really talk about line breaks without also talking about a poem's overall rhythm, and one can't talk about rhythm without at least mentioning tone, and mention of tone leads inevitably to the issue of point of view, which of course impinges on subject, and subject raises all kinds of considerations, like theme and, and, and . . .

You get the picture.

———

A poem often breaks down because its elements are *not* well enough integrated. Often it is useful to trace how and where this breakdown occurs, so that the author may attempt a more complete integration. Workshops can help in this process.

MFA graduates go forward in their work having assimilated voices that talked about their poems, that considered them from many different angles, that worried and suggested them into better versions of themselves.

Are those assimilated voices then the locus of craft? Tracing the faultlines of a poem, is that craft? What then is the difference between craft and editing? Between craft and revision?

And what about the reading of poetry by others, which teachers keep telling us is so important, is in fact crucial to a poet's apprenticeship? When we read poems are we using, or developing, *craft*?

Am I just playing with semantics?

Well. You see how I can take what should be simple and stir it into something complicated.

In the end, I suppose, it doesn't matter what we call the work we do here, both as a corporate body and as solitary makers. It is work that must be done if the poem is to become as strong as possible.

But I can think of no poorly crafted poem that succeeds as art; nor can I usefully imagine a poem that fails as art, but succeeds as craft. So the relation of craft to art in the writing of poetry is, for me, fraught. And I can rule out nothing a poet does as separate from the development of that writer's craft.

Sometimes I think that *craft* is just heightened awareness of language, a place of intensity we occupy inside the body of words.

There are things teachers can do, students can do. Exercise is good, for example. A push-up, a sestina. I like exercise. It has the advantage of forcing concentration on a task, thus opening the mind to the possibility of poetry. This necessity for sly misdirection never leaves us; it's just that after school we have to fool ourselves. "Try your best to distract yourself from what you think you have to say," as poet Patty Seyburn puts it.

Examine other poems (and other texts), current and past.

➡ Look into the "objet" poems of Francis Ponge in, for example, *The Voice of Things*, and imitate him.

> *"You have first of all to side with your own spirit, and your own taste. Then take the time, and have the courage, to express all your thoughts on the subject at hand (not just keeping the expressions that seem brilliant or distinctive). Finally you have to say everything simply, not striving for charm, but conviction."*
>
> —Francis Ponge

Other examples: Charles Simic's "Fork," Robert Bly's "The Hockey Poem," Elizabeth Bishop's "The Moose" and "The Fish."

➡ Find the most "unpoetic" text you can uncover (*National Enquirer*? Insurance regulations? Zoning codes? Political speeches?), and let it careen around in the brain until a poem begins to form, like a pearl around an irritating grain of sand.

➡ Translate a text from a language you don't speak or understand (without using a real translation) into English, by sound similarity alone. Swedish works well.

➡ Try a "negative inversion." Copy, line-by-line, a simple poem by someone you admire on the left side of a page. On the right side, invert each line to its opposite, creating your own, somewhat nonsensical lines. I bet your poem will take off after three or four lines.

Take advantage of your experience—cognitive, sensory, and emotional:

➡ *Look*, said Rodin. Go outside (or stay inside) and look at *something*, for a long time. Then, and only then,

63

"reproduce" it in a poem. In 1905, Rilke moved to
Meudon, France, to take a job as the secretary of Rodin.
When Rilke told Rodin that he had not been writing lately,
Rodin's advice was to go to the zoo and look at an animal
until he truly saw it. "The Panther" was the result.

➡ House Poem, by Lynn Emanuel: Draw a blueprint of the
first house or apartment you can remember living in.
Include, if they were important to you, the yard, attic,
basement, garage. Draw in whatever stirs your memory.
Immediately after finishing the blueprint, free-write about
this house. Act as though you are transcribing a dream.
Don't stop. You should have five to ten pages. The next
day take it out and read it; as you are reading it underline
phrases, bits of language, moments that seem interesting.
Begin to construct the first draft of your poem.

Teachers, especially since writing became "professionalized" in
the mid-twentieth century, have been wonderfully creative at devising
exercises to break up students' received notions of what poetry is, or
should be, as well as to get students to move around *inside* language
in ways that strengthen their powers of syntax, metaphor, rhythm,
etc.—all the indivisible elements that make poetry.

But there are also teachers who ask students to bring just their
poems into workshop (or private conference) and then deal directly
with what the student has made on his/her own. This can work
as well as exercises. The idea is that hopefully—and hope is always
an essential feature in this process—the result will be successively
stronger versions of the writing. Or the process will reveal a poem's
irremediable weakness and result in the poem's abandonment.
Issues of "craft" are introduced and addressed as they arise naturally
in the course of revisionary work, solidifying in the student's mind
the valuable idea that craft *is* revision.

Either approach, having students complete defined exercises

or simply responding to free-written poems, can work. I have experienced both methods inside the Revisionarium, as student and as teacher, and have seen that in the right hands either can be effective. When we're talking about teaching poetry writing, I don't think pedagogy can be separated from the teacher. There are gifted teachers just as there are gifted writers. These talents don't necessarily travel together: there are mediocre poets who are excellent teachers, and very good poets who can't teach for love or money. I don't think I know, however, of any *bad* poets who are *good* teachers. Maybe they exist too.

O, Research

Research is not the map (there is no map) . . .
—Kiki Petrosino

A recently published study in a journal called *Qualitative Research* is entitled "Expressive research and reflective poetry as qualitative inquiry: a study of adolescent identity." The five authors of this study summarize their project thusly (from the abstract): "In this study of adolescent identity and development, poetry is used as data, as a means of data representation, and as a process of inquiry."

Poetry as *data*. Wow. Whoda thunk it? Poetry, apparently, is *big* in qualitative research.

The idea seems to be that poetry may be used as an investigative tool in the field of scientific inquiry—at least, in the *social* sciences. I can find no evidence to suggest that the "data" of poetry has proven equally useful in the hard sciences. While I take a guarded, not to say dim, view of such methods in general, I won't be on the picket line at the fourth *Annual International Symposium on Poetic Inquiry*. As my grandmother used to say, if that's their idea of fun they can have it.

Before we move on to matters of research more relevant to the actual writing of poetry, *qua* poetry, I cannot resist relaying two more examples of poetry as research, two studies that uncover enlightening relation between (or as a result of) poetry and research. The first makes a stab at combining poetry and "hard" science, the second confirms what most of us moderately successful poets have long suspected:

1.

"Poetry Writing and Secretory Immunoglobulin A," G. Lowe, J. Beckett, and G. M. Lowe, *Psychological Reports,* vol. 92, no. 3, part 1, June 2003, pp. 847–8.

The method, the result:

"17 healthy students provided saliva samples for Immunoglobulin A (s-IgA)

assay before and after sessions of either writing poetry or reading magazines (control). Levels of s-IgA increased after the poetry-writing sessions, but not after reading."

2.

"The Cost of the Muse: Poets Die Young," J. C. Kaufman, *Death Studies*, vol. 27, no. 9, November 2003, pp. 813–21.

The method, the result:

This study examines 1,987 deceased writers from four different cultures: American, Chinese, Turkish, and Eastern European. Both male and female poets had the shortest life spans of all four types of writers (fiction writers, poets, playwrights, and non-fiction writers), and poets had the shortest life spans in three of the four cultures (and the second shortest life span among Eastern European writers). Possible reasons for the poet's shorter life span are then discussed.

Dear Poets, the moral: buy term life insurance, early and often. And be sure to spit in a cup immediately after writing poems. Place cup in freezer. Save those immunoglobulins for a rainy day.

But this is not what I mean by "research" in relation to poetry.

What I would like to look at is the idea that research into the world of hard facts and bodies of knowledge—especially those conventionally thought of as outside the domain of poetry—can enhance, enrich, and open out the poetry we write.

I think it's more or less understood that, in a wider sense, a poet's *research* includes every perception and experience in this life, starting with the first slip of consciousness. An alert awareness to past and present, the poet as wakeful *witness*, is essential to writing.

> *I think the trick is to pay attention; but really I'm saying what my trick is, and it's not so much a trick but a lifelong habit.*
>
> —Gerald Stern

What I'm talking about is a more focused kind of investigative fact-gathering used to broaden the poet's vision and language, to expand the container called "poetry."

Poets have been using research in this way for some time now. It's an interesting and valuable contemporary trend: welcoming into our work odd and unexpected knowledge found "outside the self."

Of course, in a sense this has always been so. Early poetries were largely indistinguishable from other intellectual disciplines, or served as nascent versions of other disciplines, carrying inside their rhythmic borders millennial histories of war and rulers, origin stories, cultural movements and changes, observations of nature, etc.

Nineteenth-century poets were curious and informed about the science of their day and attempted whenever possible to include it in their work. In fact it was expected by many Westerners of that period that science would soon solve all our questions and problems, and poets, for the most part, signed on to that program with enthusiasm. A neo-renaissance seemed plausible, a period of union of art and science. Poets and scientists often knew and socialized with each other: Keats's "watcher of the skies" was pointedly modeled on astronomer William Herschel, discoverer of Uranus. Later, during the fever pitch of "Romantic Science," Coleridge invited the extraordinary chemist Humphry Davy to set up a lab in his Lakeland home. Davy did, and the two proceeded to have a grand old time getting hammered on nitrous oxide (Davy taking notes, of course), among other perhaps more edifying shared experiences.

A history of the relationship between science and poetry would make for a fascinating book. Someone should write it. Avanti.

When I was forming myself (and being formed) as a poet in my twenties, the fields of science and poetry had amicably separated. It is difficult to imagine Strand or Merwin, as learned and urbane as they were, laboring to insinuate the latest discoveries in physics or cosmology into their pared-down, *stone and bone,* deep-image poems. And it is equally hard to imagine that Robert Creeley or Alan Dugan sat down with much more than their own minds, which lucky for them included encyclopedic knowledge of English and American prosody, to write the next poem. It is true that Adrienne Rich, Lucille Clifton, and other pioneers were bringing fresh cultural, ethnic, and gender perspectives into what was at the time a practice dominated by white men. And there was "language" poetry, which came packed with its own political theory and ambitions for wider cultural inclusion. But beyond these exceptions the era of the seventies was more romantic than classical, and the brief lyric issuing from a definable self was clearly the dominant and ascendant mode.

Everything changes. Today young poets have the speed and reach of the Internet at their fingertips. This, coupled with a postmodernist worldview that inherently distrusts the notion of a stable self, has made for an innovative and decentered poetry that allows for a sometimes bewildering range of voices, tones, rhetorical sets, "nonpoetic" disciplines and obsessions, jargons, and exotic, un-"poetic" bodies of knowledge, to be incorporated into the work. It has resulted in a restructuring of what we mean when we say *poetry*. It has made for an amazing variety of *poetries*.

There is no codification for the research methods employed by poets in the construction of poems, thank God. But there are a few specific examples I'd like to give as illustration, and some words from the poets themselves on process. I think this may help, Dear Poet, to fire up in you a passion for experimentation, such that you too consider opening your poetry to some of the neglected detritus of the world, cyber and otherwise, and particularly to those facts and disciplines that have never yet seen the inside of a poem.

I asked my friend, colleague, and fellow poet Kiki Petrosino for her thoughts on "research" in poetry. Here is how she replied:

> *My research is pretty unscientific. Right now I'm in the office, working on a new poem. So far, I've looked up information*

on skeletonization, the ancient demon Astaroth, carnivorous beetles, sunfish, the mallow plant, and the Lesser Key of Solomon. Much of this has been through Google, because I only want to know a little bit about each thing right now . . . just enough to complete an image and move on to the next line. I look something up, think about it for a few minutes, turn it over a few times in my imagination, and then test out a phrase. Undoubtedly, what I come up with has very little to do with facts and much more to do with making noise! I count Susan Howe as one of the major poets in my constellation, but I rarely devote myself to the painstaking research on single topics that she is so adept at. My method is to do a lot of jumping around (literally—moving from my desk to the computer, to the dictionary, etc.).

Kiki's informal method is, I think, the method of *most* poets, a matter of what we might call "research by association."

Poems can begin in a variety of ways: with a line, an image, a rhythm, a piece of speech, an obsessive dream, or worry. Poems can even begin with an idea, though this may be the rarest of incitements. But in most cases the actual work of the poem doesn't *really* begin until some words appear on a page. In this instance Kiki had obviously started, had already written down a few words that interested her. She looked these words up. She mulled over her findings. She delighted in parts of it, and allowed those parts to suggest further words, rhythms, lines, or targets of research.

And so she went, moving blissfully on a kind of poetry scavenger hunt, where the prize at the end is the larger mystery of the newborn poem itself. On the way, one clue leads by association to the next, and the explorer keeps moving, even though the "correct" number of clues is unknown, it's up to the poet to decide even what a *clue* is, and even some of those unearthed treasures that seemed most promising will be discarded in the final work.

Crossing a stream, rock by rock, throwing down each new stepping-stone as you go . . . which brings us to the second part of Kiki's answer, and an even better simile:

> *One line leads to another (at least, on good days), like a rope of scarves through a magician's hands. Some piece of language will come up—for example, the word "swamp," which I love. And then I think to myself, what grows in the swamp? And I remember a Workshop friend of mine, Nellie. She has this recipe for "real" marshmallows that uses the mallow plant as an ingredient. Nellie hunts the mallow in the marshes near her childhood home in the countryside. So then I look up the word "mallow" to see what comes up, not because I'm going to talk about Nellie—or marshmallows—in my poem, but because I like the sound of the word "mallow" and think it might be spooky enough to work well in this line I'm trying to write about the swamp. The word "mallow" leads me to the word "stem," and suddenly I'm thinking, "what else has stems?" And that thought eventually leads me to this line: "I hear your old jaws snag on the stem of a grin." Did I mention this is a completely arbitrary & weird process?? Research is not the map (there is no map), but it might function as a kind of compass through the field of language. A terrifically broken compass, of course.*

"I hear your old jaws snag on the stem of a grin"—an interesting line, and what a journey Kiki took to arrive at it. I really don't know of a better, more specific description of the odd and intuitive way poems may be made. In one compressed paragraph (well, now two) we see clearly how the associative process moves in many directions at once in the poet's brain—the sound of one word leads to contemplation of its literal meaning, then to all that the signified "thing itself" (*swamp*) contains. This leads to a memory of a friend whose interesting habit Kiki associates with *swamp*. Then the why of the association brings up a specific, lovely word—*mallow*—which the poet "likes the sound of." The poet then looks this word up. The results of this bit of "research" lead the poet to consider one part or implication of that word, again shifting from desirable sound to a more literal, material denotation. Finally, Kiki asks herself to think of other contexts or categories in which this last clue in the trail might appear. When she finds the right one, the line comes to her, presto—as if by magic.

Another method of "poetic research" is writ large by the work of the prolific and interesting American poet Susan Howe, whom Kiki mentioned. Howe has completed several book-length works on historical figures. The result, however, is not by any means the poetic twin of "historical fiction." Howe does obsessive, exhaustive research into the life and work of her models—but the final work includes actual as well as imagined scenes from the lives, pieces of speech, comments, and perspectives from other writers and thinkers, as well as Howe's own responses to the model's work and thought. She likes to see and feel actual objects her subjects used. Interspersed among the pages of her published poems she includes photocopies of many actual documents discovered in her research. Her method permits meditation on such figures as Emily Dickinson, Herman Melville, and Charles Peirce to raise epistemological and linguistic questions suggested by their work, but not limited to it.

She also includes her own questioning—Howe is centrally interested in language, its operations, capacities, and limits. The result is that the figures the poems investigate come off as fascinating and much more complex than any of us had thought, and their work is placed within a larger context of language and the possibilities of meaning. Still, the real star of the work may be Howe herself— her urgent interactions with Emily, dramatized in meticulous, self-questioning lines.

Here is Howe, speaking in an interview about her projects:

I need to ground my work in particulars. In my case this usually means a material object such as a book, or a manuscript, most recently lace. Often a historical moment, or a specific person. Not a made-up character—I could never be a novelist—but I try to understand all aspects of the person I am writing about the way a playwright or an actor might. Esther Johnson, Emily Dickinson, Mary Rowlandson, Hope Atherton, Anne Hutchinson, Thomas Shepard, Clarence Mangan, Herman Melville, Charles and Juliette Peirce—the only way for me to reach them, or for them to reach me, is through the limited perspective of documents. This doesn't say much about my notion of self—because for something to work I need to be another self."

We live in an age of nonfiction. Our loss of faith in the imagination is evident in the proliferation of reality-based TV shows, and the popularity of the memoir, over and against such forms as the novel and other explicitly imaginative forms (poetry?). Even popular scripted shows, like the CSI series, make exhaustive use of scientific (forensic) facts and methods, as if to assure the viewer that, *it's all right, this stuff is the way it's really done, it's* true. Prosecutors now complain that the show has embedded in the public mind the notion that every crime can be neatly solved, in every case, by DNA evidence. The verdict in the recent Casey Anthony case, in which the DNA evidence was slim and inconclusive, is instructive. Casey Anthony—the lurid, unfolding-in-real-time courtroom drama, presented as another form of reality theater . . .

Why this hunger for the factual, for "reality"? Is it because our personal experience has become so mediated, so *meta*? Many people have asked this question, and by now it's nearly a dead horse. I will not add any further blows.

But the relationship between the real and the imagined is not a new fascination. In fact, it is the same question that gave rise to the shadows on the walls of Plato's cave; it's just that we still have no answer, not even a satisfying distinction between the two realms.

What *is* new in poetry, and in the interesting genre-bending that has become a more general literary trend, is that the question is currently being raised in more explicit, concrete form, *as an expression of the work itself.*

Kathleen Ossip's recent book of poems, *The Cold War*, contains a number of smart longer poems that mix factual data of various kinds with more conventionally "lyric" language. Ossip has an apt sense of the dramatic, and these poems develop and accumulate force as they progress.

One of them, "American Myth," assembles a kind of meditation on that period of American history known as "The Cold War Era." The whole book, of course, is concerned with that period, but "American Myth" seems to me a particular crystallization of the book's themes. The poem weaves together three distinct strands, two of which are narrative and based on the lives of historical figures Wilhelm Reich and Will and Ariel Durant. The third strand takes the form of lyric interludes—brief, short-lined, and more dreamily suggestive than the denotative narrative portions. The lyric sections lead the reader toward the speculation that they issue more from the *poet's* point of view, though that is left indeterminate—the poem's author seems to prefer to keep her distance, from us, if not from the characters in the poem.

Here is what Kathleen told me about the subject of "research" and poems, as it applies to her practice:

> *I'm usually more comfortable dealing with atmospheres and sensations than irritably reaching after facts. "American Myth" began, really, when I was a kid, dipping into books I didn't understand on my parents' bookshelves. Wilhelm Reich seemed to have something to do with sex and that was a plus. The Durants as a married couple who wrote books together were intriguing, as was their huge success. Later on, when I was writing* The Cold War, *trying to figure out that period of*

history (and my parents) (and our current mess), Reich and the
Durants seemed emblematic of two vaguely opposing ways of
behaving in the world, both American to the core. But I didn't
have the facts to back up my intuition. One summer I bought
and begged for four days away from my family. I locked myself
in a motel room with a biography of Reich, some of his books,
and a joint autobiography of the Durants. There were the facts
and they were interesting enough to make a poem, which took
a prose-poemy shape. But I added some lyric interpolations,
for mystery. Fact + mystery became my stab at "reality" or
"truth."

This paragraph is instructive for several reasons. First, Ossip
reminds us that the most interesting writing, however the writer
accomplishes it, proceeds from personal obsession or passion.
This is why I think many of the current spate of "research" poems
fail—the writer was more interested in being admired for her own
cleverness than in the subject of her poem. Don't write about what
you know—write about what has made you ill with interest, what
has infected you.

Then sex (of course!). To paraphrase the Goncourt Brothers,
sex would be the most ridiculous and trivial of subjects, if only it did
not contain the secret of life. That the poem centrally features sex
Ossip wryly calls "a plus."

Then there is the necessity for sustained and concentrated
attention, especially in the case of the long poem. Ossip "bought
and begged for" time to write the poem. I find this formulation
touching; anyone who has schemed and longed for time and space
to write will empathize. I speak in other parts of this book about
the essential selfishness poets must practice, and how difficult
it is to find balance between this necessity and having a life that
includes others, perhaps even a family. There are no one-size-fits-
all answers to the dilemma, and there is no way around the need
to solve it.

Finally, we can add Ossip's equation to the others I have put in this book, in my ongoing quest to formulate the mathematics of poetry:

Fact + mystery = "reality" or "truth"

Now, go find Kathleen Ossip's poem, and read it. Look into Howe and Petrosino's books. The best way to emulate certain authors, or to absorb their methods, is to read their work, with love and hunger.

Then, open your poems to the wider landscape, especially the "unpoetic" parts. It's an enormous, fertile field.

The Private I

The poet's work is to make a private vision public—through the stubborn, inadequate, infinitely flexible medium of language.

The two main mistakes made by poets starting out are 1) to assume that private references will be clear to the reader, and 2) to assume that parts of experience are suitable for transformation into poetry while other parts are not, and that the young poet knows the difference between the two.

The first error generally becomes painfully apparent the first time the poet shows the work to someone else and receives an alert, honest response. The poet then may choose to alter the poem so that it opens into more public form, or . . . not. We are always free to hold on to our hermetically sealed, private vision. The poet who goes on to take the art seriously, however, learns to make the work "accessible" to the intelligent reader without compromising the terms of private vision.

Mistake number two takes longer to "correct," and is an even more intimate error, because there are places we've been that we simply do not want to revisit, no matter their possible value to our work, and no matter how far into life we are. On the other hand there are those experiences that should, we are convinced, be prime material for poems; and yet, when we try to write, the words turn to ash in our hands. Then there is the matter of those little bits of "trivial" experience or sensation that, to our surprise, turn into our best poems. How to know which is which, how to sort it all out?

When I was younger I made the second mistake in large strokes. I thought that my "poetry life" was in the future, and the life I was living at the time was preliminary, rehearsal for the real thing.

I was wrong. Everything I did, everything I saw and perceived and felt would later be of use to me in my poetry. I don't mean that every experience turned into a poem about that experience; I mean that it was all of use. This turned out to be especially true of what I thought of as the most "unpoetic" parts of my life. The things that happened to me while I was "in rehearsal," the things I saw and felt, were forming the subtext, the substratum of my later poems. They were forming me.

I know now that I cannot predict what will make a poem, and that there is no subject or tone within my realm of experience, past or present, that can reasonably be excluded from the possibility of my next poem.

Bobby the Ape

We were tooling down West Side Highway in one of the anonymous green Fords my father picked up at police auctions. Bobby's meaty right hand gripped the top of the wheel, swinging it back and forth with nonchalant aggression as he threaded a path through potholes and the sparse Sunday traffic.

Our subject was a professor at the New School, who our client suspected was having an affair with his wife. We were to find the professor, tail him for the day and track his movements. The wife had previously told our client she was going to spend the day shopping in the city. If the professor did hook up with the client's wife, great—we'd have a chance to get what we called "honeymoon pictures"—shots of the two *in flagrante delicto,* or at least obviously together.

Bobby flexed his right bicep and told me to punch his arm. "Go ahead, kid, give it a whack." I did. "That your best shot?" Bobby said. I wound up and socked him as hard as I could.

"Like a bladder full of wet sand, eh?" Bobby said. "I can crack a fuckin' Brazil nut in the crook of my elbow, eh?"

"You're a monster, Bobby, a fucking ape."

I lit a Marlboro and looked at the Hudson. It was a beautiful fall day and the river looked plush and slightly rounded, like the gray velvet sleeve of a medieval courtier. This of course was exactly the kind of observation that, had I been insane enough to *share* it with Bobby, would have drawn a derisive snort and a blunt question concerning my manhood.

Bobby's bulk was impressive. He was six-three, around two-fifty. His wristwatch seemed shrunken and pinched on his Popeye forearm, and the packed muscles of his shoulders and arms stretched taut the material of all his clothes. This was before big-and-tall men stores and he could not find a shirt or jacket that fit him. Or maybe Bobby just liked the effect of his muscles straining the fabric, and deliberately bought a size too small. I wouldn't put it past him.

His were not the fashionably cut or chiseled muscles of today—just huge, undefined. I don't think Bobby had ever lifted an iron plate or done a single push-up. He was just one of those archaic creatures whose physical power is an unearned part of his genetics, like his sand-colored hair, the spray of freckles across his nose, or the pale, Aqua Velva blue of his eyes.

Bobby was also fearless, and a practiced, excellent fighter. He'd grown up in a lethal neighborhood in the Bronx. On a bad day he would have beaten the crap out of an ersatz tough guy like Sylvester Stallone with one arm tied behind him. And that would've been Bobby's idea of fun.

We found a short slot on Bleecker Street, the subject's neighborhood. Bobby wedged the Ford in and stuck a *Clergy* sign in the front dash while I fed the meter to give us some initial credence. We found a pay phone that worked, and Bobby dialed the subject's number and let it ring long enough to be sure he wasn't home.

Then we began checking out the streets, one by one, Bobby walking one side while I tagged parallel with him on the other, both of us casing the windows of restaurants, galleries, head shops, etc.

We had pictures of our subject from a student bulletin we'd dug out of the library, and a few snapshots of the wife provided by the client. From the picture it appeared that our guy was out of central casting—middle-aged, tweedy, graying beard, glasses, long hair, no smile—looks that would have gotten him instantly fired from my client's law firm, but perfect for a professor at the New School.

The wife was also predictable, with her straight teeth, big, expensive hair, and the vaguely anxious smile of a monied, educated woman. An Aryan from Darien, indeed. Her kids were all out of the house and in school, and her sudden excess of free time happened to coincide with the fresh wave of the women's movement. So she had signed up for graduate studies.

Many such women came to our office, in person or through lawyers, looking to hammer their philandering husbands. Or their husbands came. In this case our client was the husband. We didn't care; we charged the same hourly rate no matter who knocked on the door. It just depended on who got to us first.

Bobby caught my eye on MacDougal and bounded across the street, stopping en route to pound his fist on the hood of a car he'd forced to stop short. He was smiling boyishly—he had made the subject *and* the client's wife having coffee together in a tony café. We'd hit pay dirt.

I was to go into the restaurant and sit with a cup of coffee. I was young, and my long hair and tattered jeans made me blend in. Bobby would wait outside, across the street, ready with the telephoto.

When people ask, because they are always curious, I tell them the best, most lifelike depiction of investigative work is the scene from *The French Connection* where Gene Hackman as Popeye Doyle is standing on the sidewalk across the street from a fancy French restaurant, stamping his feet in the Manhattan winter cold, sucking on a deli coffee and chomping a doughnut. He's waiting for The Frog, who, visible to Doyle, sits at a window table inside the restaurant, consuming a meal with great deliberation and sensual delight. I generally find reaction to this illustration is mixed: the Doyle character is sleazy, his methods coarse, racist, unglamorous. Not a shred of the darkly gallant ethics of a Marlowe, say. It is, as they say, what it is.

This particular setup was better than the norm. I got to sit in a chair in a nice joint. I chose a table in the café that gave me a view of the subjects but was off in an unobtrusive corner. I ordered an espresso and cannoli and opened the paperback I'd brought along. It was easy and effective to play the student I actually was.

I let my eyes wander in a bored way from the page to the subject and the wife. There was between them the usual laughter and furtive touching of hands one expects from lovers. Occasionally they'd get quiet and just moon at each other. In my mind, our client's suspicions were confirmed.

They seemed to linger forever. I actually got some reading done for school, while being careful to glance at them often. I had learned from experience how easy it was to drop a tail. You stare at somebody for two or three hours straight, bored out of your mind. Then you sneeze, wipe your nose, and—your man has vanished. I knew Bobby was waiting with the camera, no doubt pretending to take touristy shots of the buildings and street. Or whatever; nobody would mess with him in any case. But I didn't want to be the one to fuck up.

It wouldn't be Bobby, that I knew. No matter what else might be said about him, he was the best investigator I'd worked with. He was dogged and obsessed by whatever case he was on, and he had a beautiful line of bullshit. He could, as he often bragged, "charm the panties off a pregnant Sunday school teacher." I'd once seen him talk his way into the inner offices of a striking labor leader, when we were working for management. He came out two hours later with his arm around this one-time mob enforcer, and the guy was laughing like hell. Bobby had enough information to kill the strike in court, though as it happened the client settled before it came to that.

We had three or four other investigators on the payroll. But our lawyer clients loved Bobby, and often requested him by name. He got results.

I made sure my tab was paid, so when the wife slung her handbag over her shoulder and quickly rose I was also ready to leave. She left, but the subject stayed put. Either this was the end of their playtime together or they were being cute.

I decided to wait for the subject, hoping Bobby would think to tail the wife. We had walkie-talkies, but in those days they were huge, unusable on such a close-up surveillance. But Bobby and I both knew the professor's home address, and had agreed to meet there if we got separated.

The professor left five minutes later. I gave him a little lead out the door and then followed. He moved at a brisk pace, both hands stuffed in his jean pockets, his long hair jouncing against his sportcoat collar with each step. I saw that he was heading in the direction of his apartment.

On the way he stopped at a florist shop. I picked a *Time* magazine from a sidewalk newsstand and flipped absently to the entertainment section. He came out almost immediately, carrying a thin box trailing green tissue, and crossed in front of me to the street, nearly knocking the magazine from my hands. I wondered then if he'd made me, but not for long; he was moving fast.

He jagged swiftly around the fenders of impatiently revving cars, crossing against the light. I was a few steps behind him. Just as I got to the crosswalk the cars lurched forward like a pack of leashed hounds let go all at once. I stood there watching the professor turn the corner of the next block and disappear, my thumb up my ass.

It was always a shock to visit the home of someone I had only known at work. I avoided it whenever possible. The idea that someone I had come to regard as a function attached to a suit actually slept in a bed, or sat crumpled and weary in a chair at day's end, or opened a can of tuna fish in a harshly lit kitchen, was repulsive to me. I knew that all these intimate actions and more occurred in my colleagues' lives, but I preferred not to think of them. This was temporary, a bizarre and inelegant world, full of brutal losers. There was nothing to learn from it, nothing to take with me. I wanted no part of it, except for the flexible hours, and the money it gave me to live.

But there was one time I had to pick Bobby up at his apartment. I forget the particulars now, but it was a duty I somehow couldn't avoid.

He lived in a high-rise apartment complex in Mt. Vernon, with long, narrow, uncarpeted hallway floors of marbled green-and-black linoleum. Fluorescent lighting gave the thickly painted lime walls a sickly cast. My steps echoed, children cried out behind closed doors. The whole place reeked of Chinese takeout and cat piss. At least I hoped it was cat piss.

Bobby's wife, Kathleen, a pretty brunette with sharp features and an apologetic smile, answered my knock. I was startled by her size—she was tiny, under five feet, and delicate-boned. My first reaction was amazement that Bobby had not at some point in their marriage crushed her simply by turning over in his sleep. I stood staring at the stuccoed ceiling, mumbling some stupid compliment about the swirled pattern, unable to look the poor woman in the eye.

Bobby was in the shower, and Kathleen offered me a seat on the sofa and a cup of coffee while I waited. She must have had the coffee already made, because she left the room and returned almost instantly with two steaming china cups on saucers. She set the cups down so gingerly she might have been arranging flowers before a wake. Neither of us spoke.

The living room where we sat together balancing saucers on our knees was furnished with threadbare, obviously hand-me-down rugs, chairs, etc. A particularly bloody crucifix, red gushing from Christ's forehead and side, hung prominently over the TV, which had a paperclip scotch-taped over the peg of the missing on/off knob. Animals made of bumpy white glass and souvenir thimbles from the counties of Ireland were neatly arranged on a hanging shelf. Once-white lace doilies were precisely centered under the end-table lamps. A few gilt trophies from Bobby's high school football days tilted in the sill of the room's only window. Otherwise, all was bare necessity. I felt the sadness of an immaculate, well-ordered poverty.

I knew Kathleen was awed by my standing as the boss's son. It was obvious from her blush, her silence. And from the fact that Bobby often mentioned how he bragged to her about "his partner, the next in line, The Prince." She probably believed that Bobby's future, and therefore her future and her sons' futures, would depend upon my approval.

This was not true, of course. I had absolutely no plans to take over my father's investigative firm. Still, I felt her weighing my words as if they were gold flakes on a scale, though I did my best to keep the tone light and inconsequential.

After we had gone through the sports her sons were involved in, and the rain that had been falling for a week, and how much work I'd had to put into my second-hand Vega, I could think of absolutely nothing further to say. Kathleen, who was also at a loss, finally rose and walked to the kitchen without explanation.

Bobby emerged with wet, slicked-back hair, his big limbs pushing the scent of Brut before him into the room. He lumbered past his wife without acknowledging her presence. She didn't seem surprised. We left.

I did not see Kathleen again, and I never met her and Bobby's sons.

When I got to the subject's address, a five-story brownstone on East 16th Street, Bobby was taking the picture of some kid about twelve years old, who stood stiffly on the front stoop of the house next door to the subject's.

"What's happening?"

Bobby held one hand up to me like a stop sign, said, "Hold on," and kept squinting through the lens at the kid, who glanced toward me briefly, then turned back to the camera.

They were both in a serious mode and I didn't know yet what Bobby was up to, so I lit a cigarette and stood watching as Bobby clicked away, every so often giving a little encouragement to the kid, *That's good, Dan, good—now look the other way—right! Excellent! Dan, Dan, Dan—you're a natural!* and moving nimbly around the stoop's perimeter like a bear disguised as a fashion photographer.

"I think we got it, Dan, good work." Bobby said. "Like you to meet my assistant here, Jacques Periot." He put an arm like a lead cloak over my shoulder and guided me to Dan's outstretched hand. "Jacques, here, is from France, a very promising young director who's kind of an apprentice with our company. Jacques, Dan Abernathy."

I shook Dan's hand, which was soft and clammy with preadolescence, and smiled. Dan reminded me of a prepubescent Matthew

Broderick, except geekier. "Dan," Bobby said, "give me a moment with my assistant." Dan nodded and flashed me a goofy smile.

Bobby maneuvered me a few steps away, out of the kid's hearing. "Dan here lives in the joint next to our professor. His parents are out for the day. I gave him one of these—" Bobby handed me a business card that said *Bobby Houge, Cinematographer, Abraxis Pictures,* and listed Bobby's cousin's Brooklyn address and phone number. "We're here scouting location shoots for our next movie, OK? Dan's gonna let us onto his roof to take a few shots. You speak French?" I shook my head. Bobby thought for a moment. "That's all right; neither does the kid. That's why I made you French. Let me do the talking."

Bobby had already set things up fine—the kid led us right to the roof, and would've jumped off, too, if only we'd taken his picture in midair and promised him a bit part in the "movie." On the way up the five flights I noticed that the kid's parents had bucks—Tunisian wall hangings, old barn wood paneling—lots of real art, a Lichtenstein, one Renoir etching, I think.

The roof area was small, but fitted out like the deck of a yacht, with slat wood palletes laid down as flooring, canvas chairs, and a heavy glass-and-teakwood coffee table. A miniature herb garden flourished from the top of an old whiskey barrel. Bobby took a few more dramatic shots of the kid sitting on a cornice, framed against the downtown skyline, and then politely asked him to give us a little time alone to look around and set up shots. "Sure," Dan said. "I'll be right in my room, in case you need me," and disappeared down the ladder of the slanted hut that led below deck.

"Now what, Captain?" I said.

Bobby leaned over the wall parallel to the subject's building and looked down. He lifted the Nikon strap from around his neck and handed me the camera. "Hold this," he said, and climbed up the wall.

"Are you fucking nuts?"

It was only about three empty feet between buildings, but it was a long way down, and I was impressed at how easily Bobby cleared the space, how deftly and quietly his big body accordioned to absorb the force when he hit the other roof, and how he then rose up, smiling and dusting a bit of soot from his knees.

"Coming?"

"No fucking way."

"Throw me the camera."

I did. Bobby caught it and walked lightly to the fire escape at the back of the roof.

"Just wait there. Give Dan some bullshit if he comes out. I'll be back up soon." He hung the Nikon around his neck and started down the iron ladder.

Another case, I forget the particulars: Bobby and me sit in a company car waiting for a door to open and some nameless mark to appear, which is how a lot of investigative time oozes into billable hours.

Bobby is describing the different sounds made by a nightstick, hitting first a white, then a black skull. "*Thock!*—see, that's a white guy, *thock!*—kind of hollow." Bobby raps two fingers on the steering wheel. "*Thock!*—one shot and they're usually out. But an eggplant, you gotta clock them three, four times before it even makes an impression—with them it's like *dush*, kind of a dead sound—*dush. . . .*"

I should have been horrified, but I was not. I knew Bobby's background, though we never discussed it. He'd been thrown off the Mount Vernon police force for brutality, excessive force—he'd crippled some guy for life, in the course of a minor drug arrest. Besides, I'd heard this story before, and it was useless to wax indignant.

What I did was laugh. Since I was no part of the dreamy flow around me, I could afford to see it as absurd. Absurd, and all the same to me—the complex, seamy machinations of adulterers; the heroin addict nodding off in the interrogation room; the middle-aged gay who propositioned me in the Grand Central Station men's room; the perverse, childlike pleasure Bobby took in recounting his own cruelty . . . all the same.

_____

Bobby had to call out *Jacques!* twice before I remembered that Jacques was supposed to be my name. I got up quick then and trotted over to the ledge. Bobby threw me the Nikon and leapt back, landing with legs spread and knees bent, like some WWF version of Superman.

"How'd it go?" I asked.

"Nailed 'em." He made a fist, pumped it and grinned.

Then he grabbed the camera from my hands and began turning the film rewind, his eyes squinting at the unfair confrontation of sausagelike fingers and tiny crank.

Low cruising clouds ringed the horizon. The dome of air above us was clear, the fierce blue of a just-struck match. When I looked east, the sun glinted from millions of windows, while to the west impossibly tall shadows slanted down streets and across buildings . . . beautiful city.

The roof door banged open. Our subject, the professor, whom I had almost forgotten, stood in the sudden vacancy of the doorframe. One of his hands held the knob while the other clutched together the lapels of his green bathrobe. We didn't have to turn—we were facing him. We looked at him looking at us. His face was triangular, and red with fury, like a radish just yanked from the ground.

"Hey!" he yelled, pointing a shaky finger at Bobby. *"Hey!"*

Bobby turned his attention back to the tiny crank on the camera, which had sprung loose. He patiently resumed rewinding.

"Hey you!"

"Yeah, *professor!*" Bobby yelled back, smiling pleasantly as he pulled up the rewind button and popped open the camera's back plate. "How they hangin'?"

"Who the hell are you? What are you doing here?"

The professor moved closer to the building ledge. Both his hands shook, and the bottom of his robe flapped in the rooftop wind. His legs below the robe were white as broiled catfish. He was still staring at Bobby. I got the feeling at that point that he didn't know I was there, that everything outside the outline of Bobby's huge figure was invisible.

"Didn't you hear me?" he yelled. "Who *are* you?" He was bravely working himself into a righteous, New York rage. A chain of blotches bloomed along his bare collarbone. Hard to know whether they were the result of sexual flush, or hives.

"Who do you think you *are*, you, you, you . . . *Cocksucker!*" he spit out the word, but even so I must say it was not convincing.

Bobby pocketed the canister of film and snapped the camera shut. Only then did he look, casually, at the professor.

"Hey, professor—you kiss your mother with that mouth?"

The professor made a strange noise from the bottom of his throat, as if trying to clear it of a bit of pea soup.

"I'll call the cops!" he said finally.

Bobby laughed like a pasha. "Go ahead, call 'em. I got your mug shots all ready."

The professor hesitated. He pulled the robe close around his body, then decisively tied it with the attached belt. "I'm calling the police," he said, turning on his heel, and walked toward the roof door like a soldier carrying a dispatch from the front.

"It's this big," Bobby shouted, holding up finger and thumb. "This big, professor—I had a bigger penknife when I was a cub scout."

The professor turned back and stared for a moment at Bobby with a look of malign wonder. Bobby flashed him a shit-eating grin. "More like a Webelos, professor—you know, the thing before a boy scout? That's what you got—a little bitty Webelos. . . ."

On the street, Bobby handed a twenty to Dan, who was tongue-tied with gratitude. He put an arm around the kid and swore him to secrecy—*A location as good as this, see, is golden. We don't want Paramount or Fox to get wind of what we're up to, right?*

89

"Right!" Dan said, beaming.

My first surveillance in Manhattan, and a good day's work: we got made, but it didn't matter. Nobody died, nobody got shot. The scales were tipped back, at least a little: a few of the many who owed paid, and would soon pay more.

Later I was elected to drive us home. Before taking off, we bought a six-pack of tall Buds at a Smilers.

Is there any greater genius, I wondered, than the look and feel of New York on a fall night? The lights wrinkling across the Hudson like a sheet of cellophane. Looking in the rearview mirror, the city from the West Side Highway had the black-and-white sheen of a fifties movie, or a grand piano. I kept looking back at the island's black enamel body, its bone-white keys, polished to a rich gleaming.

Around a year after this night Bobby came to our investigative offices at three in the morning, drunk out of his mind, and fired five rounds into the walls and file cabinets. The next morning my father fired him. Two years after that I heard that Kathleen divorced Bobby, and only then did Bobby get sober and begin to straighten out. But then Bobby went off the wagon again and beat the crap out of some guy in a hotel elevator, and again he was fired.

Since then, nothing.

Bobby slumped in the passenger seat, passed out with his head against the window, snoring like a factory. Rod Stewart's "Maggie May" came on the radio, preceded by a screechy intro by Cousin Brucie. I cranked it up, and opened my window all the way. I put the pedal to the metal.

Wake up Maggie, I think I got something to say to you, I sang at the top of my lungs, head out the window. The air pouring in was filled with the musky crisp scent of leaves oxidizing into bronze and gold. And something else, too—salt water, fast flowing and purified of rot.

I thought I'd been immunized against the man snoring next to me, and Kathleen, and the professor, the wife. Who knew these imposters would stay with me on some basic cellular level, that I would someday soon learn for myself exactly how Bobby the Ape had come to degradation? Who knew my own arms would lengthen and develop a thick coat of fur, and I would roam the streets hunting for love?

It's late September and I really should be back at school.

I fished a joint from my pocket. Grass was the only vice Bobby didn't approve of. He was a different generation, old school. I glanced over . . . his eyes were glued shut, his mouth open and lax, a white fleck of spittle on his chin. He was gone.

Crossing the Bronx River Parkway I fired up the joint, sticking my head out the window to exhale. That air! I felt hugely awake, as if I could drive for the rest of my life.

TOP TEN QUESTIONS
POETS ARE ALWAYS ASKED

10. Did you ever think of writing a novel?

9. I write a little poetry too. Would you like to see it?

8. What kind of poetry do you write?

7. Will you sign my Intro to Lit slip? I need it to show I was here.

6. I love poetry, but the modern stuff goes right over my head. Why?

5. Did that thing you wrote about really happen?

4. The best was the stuff you said between poems. Did you ever think of writing that down, and publishing it?

3. Considering both the instability and polyvocality of current notions of *self* in postmodern art in general, and the inherent privilege of middle-class diction and its authoritarian structural lattice in particular—by which I of course include the hegemony of clarity—do you believe your poems and others like them sufficiently interrogate the implied lacunae of syntax?

2. Do you make any money writing poetry?

1. How did you get published?

4. DISCIPLINE (SELF)

Bad Boat, Bad Boy

They are bad boats and they hate their anchors.
—Laura Jensen

I will do my math problems without dreaming out the window
I will do my math problems without dreaming out the window
I will do my math problems without dreaming out the window
I will do my math problems without dreaming out the window
I will do my math problems without dreaming out the window
I will do my math problems without dreaming out the window
I will do my math problems without dreaming out the window
I will do my math problems without dreaming out the window

I didn't mind repetitive tasks, as long as they involved hand-eye coordination, as opposed to gross motor movements. So—I could have kept writing all day, the occasional squeak of the chalk on the board the only sound in an empty classroom. Doing the same thing over and over was just another way to dream.

And didn't I like nothing better than to throw one of those flesh-pink rubber balls up against a concrete wall two or three thousand times, catching it, throwing it back, until the ball lost that newborn fuzz and became smooth as a baby's bald head, except for a few scuffs and a grease mark here or there.

If they didn't want you to look out the window, why then did they make the whole wall a bank of windows, and Miss Smalley put me at a desk next to them, sun pouring in and over me, in the second-to-last row? Well, the second-to-last row was because my name was near the end of the alphabet. But I'd been getting report cards for years that said, "Jeffrey is obviously intelligent, but he has difficulty staying on task, and wastes too much time staring out the window when he should be concentrating." Why didn't they at some point move me to the row by the door, away from the windows? Of course, one could look out the windows from any desk in the room. It's just more obvious if you're on the other side of the room. And not as satisfying, in any case: the best is to be able to see, not only the sun and a few clouds, but also the top of the tree canopy, the branches waving, beckoning—making the wind visible. I went to many fascinating places at the invitation of trees.

And if my seat *had* been changed, I suppose I would have just found something else to stare at—the grain of wood in the desk, the blond hairs and the pores of the skin on my arm. I had discovered many paths, many ways to defocus, then to leave the premises, to travel far inside myself.

As I've said before, I'm lazy. I prefer sports like Ping-Pong or golf where you don't have to do a lot of running. My attention slides off any task I'm forced to do. I've never done well with authority figures. And to this day I have trouble concentrating, unless it's in the service of—what? Love or money? Yes. Having made it thus far in my life with minimal jail time and without undue amounts of public assistance, owning a home and two cars, keeping the same job for over twenty years, having gone to the DMV and the dentist on more occasions than I would have wished—these things prove to my satisfaction at least that I have learned to do things I don't want to do.

Therefore: I am a grown-up.

But it's different, so different, with things I *want* to do. While writing I feel like I'm in Wells' time machine, the sun going up and down outside, the vegetation in a sped-up process of alternately growing and withering, while inside the little globe containing me and my notebook all is timeless and unchanging. I often forget to eat. Sometimes I don't even notice the urge to urinate until that awareness moves to the center of my forehead and I throw down the pen and run from the room.

O, Miss Smalley—I *still* daydream! And windows are still handy portals, though of course it's better to sit on a porch in front of a forest or any large body of water, or on a broad avenue, watching people come and go, than in a classroom filled with silvery chalk dust.

In any case I have never been blessed or burdened with excessive energy. I like my sleep. I like saving the waking intensity I do have for what I most want to do. And in the end I suspect my conjectures about temperament are just an excuse.

Or perhaps lazy is just the way most people are, and those who set the world on fire are a touch less so. The tireless ones, the ones producing a book or more per year—you know the ones I mean. Yes, that's it. They churn, they accomplish. They make things happen, they change the world. And they do so as I sleep, or jab buttons on a wireless controller, or just sit there, like a bump on a log, in my comfy chair.

Screw them.

And yet, in my art at least, I am obsessed, I am a perfectionist. And most of the poets I know would also describe themselves in the same way, I think. How can such opposite tendencies—laziness and perfectionism—coexist in one person? (I'm *not* saying all my friends are lazy; just me.) How do they come together to make a moderately successful poet?

I'd best speak for myself.

The chore I hated most of all was mowing the lawn. It wasn't a large lawn but there were too many shrubs and trees interrupting the straight line one would wish for in mowing, and the yard was enclosed by a rail fence, an immovable obstacle surrounding the whole damn thing. A power mower would've been cool, and I think I would have jumped at mowing the lawn with one of those babies. At least for the first two or three times. My friends would have gathered around, impressed with the noise and power and danger of the large blade whirling underneath the metal hood, sharp enough to take off a few fingers, or a hand. One of my pals would have heard a story of some poor kid that actually happened to, and we would all stand around silent for a moment after he told it, imagining what it must be like to go to school—to go through life—with one hand, and a scary white stump where the other used to be. And I know I could have done a Tom Sawyer on my friends and let each one try it for a swath or two until the lawn was done, and me not sweating, not having lifted a finger except to start the engine, which was one of the coolest parts anyway. But few people in the neighborhood had such luxuries as power lawn mowers and the possibility did not even occur to my father. So I used our old wood-handled hand mower, a crotchety antique that, no matter how many times I oiled it, felt like pushing a cart filled with concrete through mud.

The worst part though was that split-rail fence, with its two longitudinal rails that fit into evenly spaced posts—twenty of them, maybe—marking the border of our little yard. My father preferred that I mow first, and then cut the grass under the rails, which were too low for the mower to clear, with hand shears. The other alternative, second in his mind but allowable, was to at some point remove the lower rails, mow underneath, and then replace the rails.

But each of these methods was a pain in the ass, and of course I did not want to do either. I spent hours trying to invent a third, easier way to mow the lawn. I devised and drew up plans for a complicated series of pulleys I could operate from a central command center, which, my theory went, would raise each bottom rail just enough for the mower to clear without me having to remove them, without even having to pause in the mowing. I tried to fashion a scythe from a broken hedge-clipper blade I found in the junkyard, which I attached to a broomstick. These and all the other schemes I planned and tried to execute failed, and inevitably I ended up mowing the lawn by sweat and by hand.

My father inspected my work, and was unyielding in his insistence on a job done right. There were no small jobs, he would say, only small men.

But, I thought, couldn't a large man also do a crappy job? For an incipient poet I had the most literal of minds. I think this is why I was often mistaken by my father and others as a wiseass.

My methods and inventions did not impress him, nor did my objection that because of this grueling, needlessly labor-intensive duty I was missing a valuable period of socialization with my peers. I don't think I put it exactly that way. But it was true—I was missing uncounted games of triangle and stickball, Ping-Pong and boomerang and Slip-n-Slide and electric football and so on.

"If you spent as much time doing the damn chore as you do trying to find a way out of it you'd be done in half the time," he said.

I considered this, solemnly, for a long time. It baffled me.

Many of the things my father said baffled me, though I tried not to let my confusion show. My father's homey aphorisms had the effect of putting the brakes on my usually swift, continuous, free-range train of thought.

When I was seven and we finally got TV and I desperately wanted to watch some show I had carefully highlighted in the *TV Guide*, for example, and for some reason my father disapproved, he would say, "If you don't see it you won't miss it." WTF? I remember thinking, decades before the acronym was born.

"If you spent as much time doing the chore. . . ." I turned the thought over and over in my mind, and at some point finally understood, or thought I did. I had to concede inside myself that what he said was in some strict sense true. But I also thought the truth of it was far, far beside the point.

In retrospect my father taught me more than either of us knew. First, I could use stubbornness to refuse to obey, even if I knew my cause was hopeless. It turns out that willingness to defy, and to accept the consequences of defiance, has uses greater than the avoidance of some loathsome chore. It was worth a lot to know I had that in me. One can, it turns out, fashion stubbornness into the more useful and socially admired *perseverance*.

The other thing my father's toughness taught is *care for a job well done,* even if the job is considered by others as trivial or unimportant.

This comes in handy when writing poems. The tendency extends.

Even now some pride of craft kicks in when I wash the dishes or vacuum the house. I like the difference I make. And I have come to a place where I am not even sure anymore which tasks *are* the important ones. Who knows, if I clean a toilet so that it whitely gleams and the next person that uses it gets the subconscious *frisson* that the world is a little fresher, a shade more worth living—or even if she's just not disgusted—who knows what this small task will be worth in the final accounting? Less or more than some mediocre or even bad poem I spent hours writing? (I hold tightly to the belief that writing a *good* poem is more valuable than cleaning a toilet. But I would not bet the ranch on it.)

Further lessons of discipline: it turns out that even in those activities we most want/like to do, like writing poetry, there are moments, or whole periods or portions of the task that are as much drudgery as roofing a house on a hot day. The only words that come are stupid, or opaque. Revision becomes a dark thicket where the choice of punctuation or the infinitude of word choice defeats us, and we are lost, incapable of deciding on the aptness of a single comma. Or every poem we write seems a pale version of a better poem by someone else or, worse, an earlier poem of our own.

Or grief and loss have hollowed out that center of self, and poetry seems a small thing in comparison. The vision of the world that once allowed poems to joyfully rise from our bodies has developed a foundational crack.

Or rejection has had a long, unbroken run, and as a result the confidence necessary to fill a page with words of any kind has steadily eroded.

Talent or desire won't touch these times. Not really. It becomes a character thing.

This may seem painfully obvious, but when young, and some-times for many years, the poetry comes as if of its own accord, easy, unconstrained. To paraphrase Rilke, the voice forces out the song. It seems as if this will last forever.

———

My father's toughness took up residence inside me, it colonized me, it grew into the force that moves me forward when my natural tendency is to hold still. It is the part that enables me to define the ground where I stand, then to protect that ground with cunning and resolve.

I realize now that the voice of Phil Levine too–his manner, his personality, his presence, the force of his love coupled with absolute intolerance for bullshit—was just what I needed to commit to a life in poetry. It was an incarnation of what I grew up with, that I had loved and feared all through my life. I recognized it immediately. Phil was the poetry version of my own father; he was my *poetry father.*

What a gift this dual legacy has been for me! The father's toughness: counterweight to the dreamer. Dreaming brought me into poetry, and it continues to keep me close to the immaterial source beneath appearance. But father toughness is what allows the dreamer to make things that are strong enough to survive. It has become my editor, my drill sergeant, my stern priest, my businessman, who must make a profit in order to live. It is bound into the craftsman who dispassionately and expertly shapes the raw material, because he has the skill to do it, and because that is what he does.

The Revisionarium

Revision 1.0

The moderately successful poet tinkers, but does not linger. The moderately successful poet moves on: to the next image, the next sound, the next line, the next poems, the next book. Poems are not perfected (perfection is possible in neither the life nor the art, in Auden's revision of Yeats). Finished, or abandoned, perhaps. The moderately successful poet makes a sign and puts it over the computer screen: DONE IS BETTER THAN PERFECT!

It is a help.

Speaking of Auden: in addition to being one of the perhaps five most intelligent twentieth-century humans, he is also among the sad cadre of poets who have revisited his early poems and hacked away at them, with disastrous results. Marianne Moore is another.

Since most poets are extremely stubborn, there is in this process of letting go the opposing force of wanting to get it right. It is an inescapable dialectic: the poet must be determined to get the poem right, to work on it until not a space or letter is changeable, but still have it remain alive. And when is that? Sometimes, many times, there is no clear answer to this question.

Revision 1.1

1. **One section or line of the poem will not behave.** Try *removing* it. If that alone doesn't work, remove it and free-write in the absence it leaves. Don't worry about matching the rhythm or tone of the other parts. You can edit the free writing later. If this doesn't work, put the poem away for a while and go on to the next thing.

2. **You have gotten the poem to a point where nothing seems wrong.** All the images, tones, speech fragments, etc., cohere, but with each revision the poem seems to have gotten deader. This is the sign that you have spent too much time with the

poem. Take one last look at your *first* draft. Try to pick out the living parts. Can you remake those parts once more, quickly? If not, put the poem away and come back to it later, way later.

3. **You can't find the poem's rhythm.** You've tried making the lines three beats, five beats, eight beats, and so on. You've tried giving each line a varied number of beats. These days with computer editing such reformatting is easy. If you've done this work and the rhythm remains elusive it may mean that what you're struggling with *wants* to be prose—a prose poem, or "creative nonfiction" perhaps; or something between poetry and prose. . . . Try forgetting about lineation entirely, and cast the piece in prose. Do you instantly see places where you want to cut, or write more? Often this is the case—the prose version suggests fresh paths of revision. Go ahead and do these revisions. Does the whole now feel more comfortable with the sound of the sentence than rhythm of the line? If so, maybe you've got yourself a prose poem. But if these operations don't lead to a new, more confident understanding of what the poem wants to be, put it away, and move on. You can always return to it later.

4. **You have misplaced the emotional emphasis of the poem.** This may accompany any of the previous problems, or it may appear on its own. Ask yourself if the scene you have set—the literal level of the poem—serves the emotional center of the poem. Or does it instead lead the reader off on tangents that, in the end, serve nothing but their own interest as flashy but isolate bits of language. To answer these questions you must first determine what the emotional center of your poem is. Once you have identified this element, you can easily measure the rest of the poem against it. One wants this primary force, or emotional emphasis, to be *equally present in all parts of the poem.* Poems are swift and sleek verbal objects, and there just isn't time or space in the universe for still more clever

language dithering in the land of self-indulgence. "Murder your darlings" (Sir Arthur Quiller-Couch). This is not to say that the poem should be a blunt instrument used merely to bludgeon the reader into feeling. What we are after is the creation of a feeling milieu, in the form of language, which includes many effects other than the emotional. But, as Pound said, only emotion endures. Poems in which the feeling is indistinct or weak or missing are, in the end, trivial.

Revision 1.2

Revision is the process a poem endures to become its best self.

Or, if you are the poet, *you* are the process a poem endures to become its best self.

Endures because a first draft, like all other objects in the universe, has inertia: it would prefer to stay where it is. The poet must not collaborate.

Best *self* because the poem is more like a person than a thing, and does not strenuously object to personification.

Yo, poem . . .

But let's not get carried away. It's your poem and you can treat it as you wish; sweet-talk it; push it around if that's what it takes. We may, if we dare, think of words as actors, and ourselves as directors. As Alfred Hitchcock notoriously said of the actors in his movies, "They are cattle."

The poem *will* resist. Besides talent, often much more than talent, a poet needs a strong *will*.

And not just for wrestling with a draft. Also to withstand failure, rejection, insults, praise, successes, blank periods, solitude, no solitude, the normal losses of any life, the inconvenience of making a living, etc. In the end, you will be known by what you have made.

Revision is the process poets endure to become their best poems.

The Silence of the Iambs

'Twas brillig, and the slithy toves
Did gyre and gimble in the wabe.
—Lewis Carroll

All students hunger for discipline, whether they know it or not. But what kind of discipline is valuable for the poet? How important to a poet's development is prosody, the study of such matters as meter and verse forms? What kind of knowledge is essential, and what is not?

It's good to know that the lines above from "Jabberwocky" are written in iambic tetrameter. And it would be sweet to carry around in your head the fact that some scholars believe Carroll's poem was at least partly inspired by Shakespeare's *Hamlet*, particularly the lines: "The graves stood tenantless, and the sheeted dead / Did squeak and gibber in the Roman streets." It's probably necessary for a poet to know that an iamb is a unit of rhythm consisting of an unstressed syllable followed by a stressed syllable. That poet will also know that much of English verse is composed of iambic pentameter, and that this is a comfortable rhythm for our language, almost a default pattern. And the poet will probably be aware of W. C. Williams' vow to "break the back of iambic pentameter."

Knowledge for its own sake is a worthy human diversion. As Vladimir says in *Waiting for Godot*, "It passes the time." (Actually, I believe he was referring to the possibility of hanging himself in order to get an erection. But the point is the same, roughly.) And knowledge that relates directly to one's art cannot help but be valuable. That's just common sense, right?

Yes. And, O! If you are sitting in a roomful of poets and the subject of oral poetry comes up and you happen to be an expert on the subject and able to give a concise and accurate précis of contemporary scholarship on the relation of skaldic verse to freestyle rap, your stock will rise. You *may* notice a dark shade creeping across the faces of some members of your audience. Ignore it. Or, if you confess in *modest* terms that you have studied Thomas Campion's ideas on classical quantitative verse, and hold forth (*modestly*) on Campion's noble but doomed attempt to fit English verse to Latin measures, you may see most of the other poets in the room silently slinking away, with furrowed brow and gnashing teeth, to Wikipedia fact-check your arrogant, modest ass. Or let's say you're an experimental poet for whom the whole idea of received prosody of any kind is deadly horseshit, and you proceed to unpack a trunkful of witty and clever anecdotes to slyly illuminate this view, while at the same time exposing to ridicule the opposition's unhip, reactionary politics. Yeah, let's say, in some universe, these things might happen. . . .

But knowledge for its own sake, at least in case of dynamic *actions* like writing poetry, doesn't cut it. There is knowledge, and there is practice. It's the latter that counts in the arts in general, and poetry in particular.

The requirements of received form can discipline the mind. Poets inquiring into the sonnet immediately begin to connect with a long line of previous makers. When they actually go ahead and attempt a sonnet, the difficulties of satisfying the form and at the same time saying *something* that does not sound entirely stupid will teach them an immense amount about language. When one has a certain number of beats to reach a proscribed end rhyme, and one is also trying to maintain a reasonably clear description or argument, the workings of English syntax, tone, and diction are brought brutally into focus. The poet learns by a combination of submission and willfulness just how form and content are related, how closely related they really are, and how magically the one may transform into the other. The discipline of form, the attempt to master prosody through *practice*, can be invaluable to a poet's development. It is a discipline, whether transmitted through teacher or self-imposed, to be embraced.

In any gathering of poets there's bound to be one or two who really have the arcana of prosody down cold, and are eager to express that knowledge, since it doesn't often come up as a subject for conversation anywhere else. Some want to talk about it because it's genuinely of interest and use to them. Their knowledge is undergirded by passion. Others use it as a cudgel to beat into cowed silence those who may, in fact, be superior poets.

The silence of the iambs.

My own feeling is that, beyond practice, knowledge of prosody is but one of countless things that may assist a practicing poet. It may indeed be a plus for a poet to have handy a copy of the *Princeton Encyclopedia of Poetic Forms,* and to know the formal characteristics of the sestina, pantoum, sonnet, triolet, etc. But it may be equally important for a poet to have, for example, a basic understanding of or at least exposure to quantum entanglement, and a few other developments in twentieth- and twenty-first-century physics. That a poet is interested in and knows about the variety of Civil War uniform buttons might turn out to be just the scrap of knowledge necessary to finish a line or complete a stanza. Or, perhaps, initiate a whole sequence of poems. Knowing something about Tarot cards, for example, sure came in handy for Eliot. He didn't know everything about Tarot cards: he knew enough.

Two things related to the study of prosody are, however, essential to the making of a moderately successful poet. The first is the assimilation of *embodied* prosody, by way of reading as much of English verse as possible, preferably at an early stage of apprenticeship. Nothing can substitute for the experience of *das Ding an sich,* the more *Ding* the better.

Of course, poets read poetry a little differently than the casual reader, or the scholar. They will imagine the poem as something they themselves had written, will try to place themselves in the "maker consciousness" of the original poet. Reading Thomas Campion's poem "Followe thy faire sunne, unhappy shadowe," for example, reading it again, and again, digesting it, making it part of the poet's body, doing the same with hundreds or thousands of poems in the English tradition—this is the study of prosody that most directly enlarges and enriches a poet's powers of composition. This is what I mean by assimilation.

After many years of such intense reading (and *reading*, again, seems an inadequate verb for what a young poet does), the poet has absorbed, on a cellular level, a whole databank, a warehouse of three-dimensional linguistic maps, a veritable doorstopper fake-book of poetic resources. After such immersion the poet *knows* what has been done and how, and is free to use, imitate, adapt, freshen, parody, invert, subvert—at will—with this internalized library of prosodic patterns and effects.

This reading, is it pleasure or study? Is it passion or discipline? It is all of these things. It is the student seeking the discipline necessary, not out of drudgery or duty, but out of love.

The second essential is related, and proceeds from the difference between the kind of knowledge I'm describing and the knowledge that results in more talk or writing about the *subject* of prosody. For serious, moderately successful poets the most compelling demonstration of their prosody is their own newly composed poems. The process of composition itself is what most engages and expresses all they have learned about the ways in which language has generated poems in times past, and how it functions in a poem newly come to being. They know they are part of a tradition, and that their labor is to add to and extend that tradition.

All poets prove their knowledge of prosody best through the poems they write. That's a lot of *P*s, but you get what I mean. Don't let them scare you with talk. Talk is just air moving in one direction or another. Don't cower, and don't be afraid to leave the room if the air gets thick.

Talk doesn't cook rice (Chinese proverb).

Over the course of a life in poetry there will be days and years when you are bursting with poetry, when you feel you have gained a mastery you will never lose, that *anything* you say will be poetry. And then there will be, perhaps, weeks or even decades of silence, periods of inner vacancy, a sudden cruel awkwardness in your relation to language itself. If you stay long enough in the art you are likely to have *every* feeling and thought possible about your work, and your place in it.

In the end what we have thought and felt, as well as what we know, is irrelevant. Knowledge and talk of poetry fades away, as do lists of publications, awards, fellowships—the whole PoBiz package. What we leave behind is our poems, and all that we knew of poetry will be clearly evident there, *in the poems.* Our discipline will be there too, hidden beneath the words.

"Form looks for content, content looks for form," Auden said. When they meet, *voilà*, we have a poem. But poets know this search is less the result of magic than of directed, intense action. It is a discipline involving the *persistence* of practice, the insistent and continuing—poem by poem, year by year—foray into language. It is silent, solitary work, of no possible interest to the outer world. And yet it is the center of a poet's work and worth as a poet.

Poems written: the great equalizer, the only evidence that counts for all claiming the title of poet. No matter how intimidating the reputation, how long or colorful the life, how learned, voluble, or original the *talk*. It's the *poems.*

Very egalitarian. And a damn good thing, too.

The Time Clock

You did the keys while carrying a heavy round metal clock encased in leather, with an attached shoulder strap. The keys were located throughout the building in small metal boxes on chains, and you'd open the key box, take out the key and turn it inside a hole in the clock until you heard a nice, satisfying click. This was the sound of the key making an impression on a paper tape within the clock that advanced with the passing minutes and hours. When a road supervisor visited the site, he would open the clock with a key only he had, and remove the tape. Then he'd check to see if rounds had been properly done and, if so, attach the completed tapes to his shift report. These reports eventually found their way to the client.

In addition to my investigative work, I took part-time jobs as a guard in my father's company, Gleason Plant Security. I covered shifts at locations from the industrial park office buildings of Greenwich to the steel foundries of Bridgeport, and everything in between. My father encouraged this, I later found out, because he harbored some hope that I would one day take over the business, and he wanted me to get firsthand experience in all the different kinds of facilities we guarded.

But my base assignment, and the one I preferred above the others, was the 4 PM–12 AM shift at the Pitney Bowes Mail Service Division (MSD) in Norwalk, housing a combination of white-collar workers of various levels and duties as well as a separate, blue-collar manufacturing area where various components of the mailing machines were fashioned and assembled. It was a round-the-clock, two-guard facility, with a guardhouse at the rear entrance where all employees were required to enter and show their IDs. Between the hours of 6 PM and 7 AM the guards were responsible for hourly key rounds, a circuit of thirty-two key stations that forced the guard to at least pass by every square inch of the place. Each round took about forty minutes to complete, and thus the necessity for two guards—

one manning the entrance while the other was generally elsewhere in the building on some stage of his round.

All the security guards I worked with on the 4–12 had stories. It was not a job for the upwardly mobile. In fact I often wondered where our employees lived; it was difficult to imagine how they could afford to buy a house on a guard's hourly wage, or even pay rent, anywhere in Connecticut. But of course there were *those* parts of town, as there were in every city, even the most posh. Even in Greenwich, which at various times has been listed as the richest township in America, someone had to take out the garbage. Someone had to mow the lawns. And someone had to guard the limestone, concrete, marble, and steel buildings the owners of the garbage and lawns and pools and carriage houses worked in, doing jobs of their own that paid well enough to live in their Connecticut, *the real* Connecticut, the one in movies and TV shows, the one that had entered the collective American imagination.

Most guards were either young and en route elsewhere, like me, or old, retired, and filling the hours of their day and the anemic digits of their pensions with an undemanding gig. The guys of in-between age—thirty to sixty, say—were generally damaged in some significant way, usually by alcohol or drugs. Or they had mental problems that had gotten in the way of more lucrative, sophisticated work. Or they were transients, drifters. Or they were men whose situation spanned these categories, including them all.

Don H. was different. He had more mind than he needed. I happened to be working in the office the day Don came in and filled out an application. When I read it before interviewing him I was stopped by what occupied his "Education" blanks (which normally remained blank on our completed forms): undergrad at Harvard, medical degree from Penn. It was safe to assume, I thought, that this was the first application at Gleason from a Harvard grad (though one of our supervisors, John Daniels, *had* graduated from Dartmouth; John was of course a drinker). I took the interview myself. I was very curious to hear Don's story.

He was a retired dentist from Wilton, a wealthy town inland from Westport (where Paul Newman lived). Retired and bored, Don just wanted something to do. He would work anywhere, he said, though he preferred to be close to home. He didn't care about the money.

Don was cleanly and tastefully dressed. He spoke with confident, fluid articulation, and without pretension. Such people sometimes approached us to employ an investigator to follow a cheating wife or husband, or to polygraph some employee they suspected of embezzlement. But such people did *not* come to our office wanting a job as a security guard.

I didn't trust him.

But neither could I refuse to hire him. If he was legit—not an ex-con or child molester—he could be *very* valuable. He would be perfect for one of our high-end corporate headquarter jobs, where executives demanded reception security people be mannerly, discrete, and intelligent. This was always a tall order, even at the high end of our pay scale. Don H., if he were for real, could work any of our jobs.

So I fingerprinted him, had him fitted for a uniform, hired him. I sent the prints to the FBI and did the telephone reference checks myself. Everything came back clean, and glowing. It looked like he was exactly who he said he was. I started him out with the 4–12 shift at Pitney Bowes.

Don learned the thirty-two key stations in one round. And after working with him at MSD I learned a few things about Don. He liked opera and naïve art (he had to explain to me what that was) and made the trip into New York twice a month for a culture fix. He talked dismissively about his job as a dentist. His clientele were mostly rich old ladies. Lots of salvage work. Good money. But after a few years most dentists don't care *what, how, who,* Don said—one mouth was much the same as the next. He certainly felt that way. In the last few years he could hardly push himself to get up and go to the office, which was why he chose to duck out early. He had enough money. He'd had enough of looking at teeth.

Though he loved the arts especially, Don could talk about any subject with intelligence. His mind was wide open. The one exception was his romantic life. He had never married, that was clear. He did not mind saying that. But I never knew if he lived alone now or had a roommate or partner, or ever had. Or anything at all about his home situation. When such things came up in conversation Don deftly steered our talk elsewhere. He never spoke of women in the two ways I was used to hearing around the office—either a world-weary, resigned, *You know the wife* kind of way, or a bluntly sexual manner typical of ex-cops and investigators. For Don it was neither. Don didn't talk about women at all.

I don't remember how poetry first came up, whether it was because I was talking about what I did at Columbia, or Don had noticed and remarked on some book of poems I'd been reading during a shared shift, or some other reason. But we did talk then about poetry, Don admitting he knew little beyond what he'd learned in college (which was more than what I'd learned in college), but going right ahead anyway and saying insightful things about the poets and poems he did know, or the ones I gave him to read right there in the guard shack, opening a book to one that knocked me out and giving it to Don to read while I did my key round, talking about it when I returned.

One day Don said, "Do you know of a poet named Robert Bly?"

"Oh yeah," I said. "He's terrific. Both his poems and his essays about poetry and his translations and his goofy, provocative theories about poetry—Robert Bly is great. How do you know him? Have you read his work?"

"He's my cousin," Don said.

Blimey! I would have exclaimed, if I'd been Australian. But me being me I sat quietly stunned. Several theatrical beats went by. I swayed.

"Say again?" I said.

"He's my cousin," Don said again.

"No, *really*," I said.

113

"*Really* he is," Don said. "Really is, my cousin."

"Whoa. Where, and how," I said. "Do tell. Tell me everything."

And Don did. I don't remember who he said the uncles and aunts all were and how they fit together but there was no question from the family tree Don sketched out with easeful familiarity, and some of the details of Bly's life I recognized as accurate from reading about him, and many others I hadn't heard but sounded credible to me because so odd and particular—cousin details, like which freckled girl cousin Bly had a crush on in the years before the war, and exactly how he cheated at games played in open fields—Don H. really was Robert Bly's cousin. And Lordy, I thought—if Don told me he had shared an informal repast of monkey brains au jus with Albert Schweitzer in the Congo one muggy night I could not have been more amazed.

Listen, Don, I said, what can you tell me about Bly's wound? His wound? Don asked. What on earth can you mean, his wound? Well, I said, Bly talks in his essays about a time in his life—his twenties, I think—when he suffered some sort of wound and was totally lost, when he had to live very simply and stay away from people. It was a mysterious period of healing essential to his development as a poet. But he never says what exactly the wound was. The implication is pretty clearly that it was more psychic than physical. Do you know what he meant?

Don smiled wryly. Well, he said, no. I don't know. But if Robert had some type of "wound" and had to go off by himself he probably did it in style. What do you mean, I asked. Robert's never had to work a day in his life, Don said. There's always been family money. So whatever catastrophe he suffered did not include poverty, I can tell you that. Wow, I said. That's not in any of his essays. No, Don said. Robert doesn't like to talk about it.

This was new information. I would have to let it sit. I would have to mull it over. I liked what Bly had said about his "wound," because I felt vaguely that I was going through something similar, at that very time. It was good to know that a big-deal poet could confess to a dark period, to speak of it in near-religious terms, to call it necessary. It gave my current state of depression and degradation a certain poète maudit glamour; it credentialed my sadness. But, unlike Robert Bly—apparently—I was earning just enough money to pay the rent and eat, and buy books and booze. My "wound" lacked the balm of a trust fund. I couldn't decide if this made my situation more or less romantic. But I did feel as if someone had just picked my pocket.

I also became friendly with a Pitney Bowes employee named Lewis. The friendly *Good evenings* I shared with other employees as they left the building for the day turned, with Lewis, into lengthening exchanges of banter. Gradually he began to park his briefcase and overcoat on the guard desk and lean against the doorframe as we talked for fifteen minutes or more while employees filed by and the building emptied out.

Lewis was a patent attorney for the company, though he was only some five years older than me. He also had a wife and two young kids. From the beginning he seemed fascinated by the fact that I was a security guard who was getting an advanced degree in poetry-writing from Columbia. Poetry was so far from law, I figured, it must have seemed exotic to Lewis. He was an avid reader of novels, *real* novels, and we discussed books by Mishima and Cheever and Malamud and Bellow. Like many otherwise good readers he claimed complete ignorance of contemporary poetry and asked for suggestions. I brought in books from my poetry library and lent him Strand, Merwin, Glück, Plath, Kinnell, Bishop, others. We would discuss each book when he brought it back, and I was surprised at how his comments and questions on the poems would sharpen my own thinking. He was, after all, not an "expert." In fact Lewis talked about poetry from the perspective of an intelligent man who had nothing to do with the academy or the arts. It was different talk than what I was used to at Columbia, that was sure. Lewis was not afraid to ask a question that would have struck my workshop peers as deathly naïve; they would have lit themselves on fire before asking such a question in class. But I was struck by the fact that they were the same questions that flickered up in many of our minds—they did in mine, I know—but were immediately beaten down by the most terrifying of all academic fears, the fear of *appearing stupid.*

When Lewis talked about some line he liked or that troubled him or made him laugh or puzzled him he said it in such plain English its straightforwardness and brevity often made me laugh out loud. *Why are you laughing?* he would ask. And I would say because I *knew* that about the poem, what you just said, but had never heard it expressed out loud in so few words and so simply. "You're a *mensch*," I would say. "A poetry mensch." This Lewis understood and was flattered by, and he smiled.

So in a brief amount of time I had met two people working as a security guard who were very, very smart and liked reading poems as long as they had a little guidance, but did not themselves write poetry. It would not be until much later in my life that I realized how rare such people were, and how much poets wished their poems would find many readers exactly like these two men.

One night Lewis stopped by the guard shack and said, "Do you have a minute? Let me show you my office." I already knew where his office was because I had tromped through every part of the building a million times and after getting to know him had noted Lewis's name on a door during one of my rounds. But I got up innocent and curious, the way a good part of me still was in those days, and said *Be right back* to Mike, who was on duty with me, and followed Lewis to his office.

Once we got there Lewis said, "Here's the typing paper and here's the drawer with Wite-Out and here's the stack of carbon paper. You can see my IBM Selectric. I know you know how to use it. And I *want* you to—to use the typewriter and my office and all the stuff in it, whenever you want. Come in every night and spend your whole shift here if you like. Hell, the chair isn't half bad for sleeping, if you feel like it." "Man, Lewis," I said. *"Really?"* "Yeah," Lewis said. "I like the idea that maybe new poems will come rolling out of my typewriter. Use it all. Let me know if you need any other supplies and I'll make sure you get them."

At this time I was married to Elizabeth and the marriage was not going well. We lived in an attic apartment in Norwalk and every night when I got off my shift I'd hurry to one of the crustier neighborhood bars where shots were cheap and order boilermakers, hammering them back until the bar closed. I didn't speak to anyone. I was not there for fun, I was there for the important business of oblivion. Human contact was very much beside the point. This was no episode of fucking *Cheers*.

After I'd squeezed full measure out of *Last call,* I'd go home and fall into sleep as if really falling, and get up when I had to, either to catch a train to Grand Central and a subway to Columbia, or to work at the Gleason office.

We would see each other, Elizabeth and I, sometimes in the afternoon when she came home from her job teaching middle school Spanish, and on weekends. Sometimes I would see her in the morning if I woke up in time. What I liked best was not to speak to Elizabeth but to pretend to still be sleeping and to watch her with slit eyes dress and get ready for work. She had a very pretty face and a voluptuous body, and I often wondered why these attributes did nothing to save us from the bitter fights and the huge wrongness lodged at the center of our marriage.

Our apartment was hung with pictures hiding the holes I'd punched in the drywall. I was lucky, I guess, my fist never found a stud. One night during an argument Elizabeth threw the Gibson acoustic guitar I'd had since I was fourteen to the floor, then brought her foot down through it, to the accompaniment of a jangly dissonant chord. Another time she jumped on me like a wild animal, her nails clawing, and I pushed her away with all my strength. She flew through the air and her head hit the edge of the sofa, her bottom teeth slicing through her lip. It was minutes before my shift, and I called the office and told them I was sick and wouldn't make it. I drove Elizabeth to the emergency room, she holding a bloody washcloth to her mouth, me wearing my silly guard uniform—clip-on tie, gold stripe down the outside of each blue pant leg. I sat with her a long time on the steel bench in the emergency waiting room, waiting for someone to sew up my wife's mouth. It's possible, I suppose, that I have felt more humiliated and guilty and ashamed all at once at some other time in my life. But I doubt it.

If I could go back I would. I would save Elizabeth from me, the young male poet with his head up his ass. I would stop the acceleration of my drinking before it was too late and the process of addiction had reached an irreversible point. But why, even if I could go back, would my younger self listen to *me*, now a grandfather, and so far, far removed in time and space? The fact is that even when I finally removed myself from the morass of self-pity and lying and unspoken sorrow that was the marriage of Jeff and Elizabeth and my life got better, much better, still I drank. Because by then that's what I did, what I was. Farmers farm, fishermen fish, drinkers drink. I was a drinker.

But I can't go back. Neither can you. Worse—you can't go back to *any* location, *any* point in the past. The arrows of time move in one direction. Hawking, the robot-voiced guy in the wheelchair, says so. You can never return, not even to the most beautiful, or most mistaken of moments.

And you know what? I think poetry does not like this state of affairs. I think poetry wants to rise up and say, *No, I am going back. Try and stop me.* And even if the poetry succeeds in this quest, as I think it sometimes does, the poet never does.

Art is feeble reclamation, but it's all we have.

One evening when I came into the guard shack, Don was already there on duty and a manila envelope lay on the desk, addressed to Don.

"There it is," said Don. "There's what?" I asked. "Your poems, back from Robert," Don said.

My heart filled then with excitement and hopeful anticipation. Is that wrong, to say "hopeful anticipation"? It's been said a billion times in the past and is one of those clichés writing teachers tend to asterisk in student writing and then in the margin write, "cliché—something fresher?" But really, when I saw Robert Bly's handwriting on that envelope and knew that he had actually read my poems and there was probably a letter or something inside discussing my poems (*Robert Bly, one of my heroes! Discussing my poems!*) my big dumb heart beat faster, started up its own little parade in fact, until it was itself a cliché. And so if I were my own student I think in this one case I would let "hopeful anticipation" slide. You don't have to be new every damn second of your time on earth.

I picked up the envelope and felt a small charge of electricity pass into my fingers. Bly's handwriting was as bold and confident as his poems. I bet he writes in longhand, I thought. Then I turned the envelope over and began to open it but suddenly stopped short. It would be better, much better, to read Bly's words later, I thought. When I was alone. Better to savor Bly's response in solitude, which Bly himself wrote about so eloquently. I would take the envelope with me on my round and open it in Lewis's office.

I made small talk with Don but attended to nothing either he or I said. Anticipation completely filled my consciousness. When the time finally came to do my round, I shouldered the clock and zoomed out of the shack with the envelope tucked under my arm. I felt like an explorer, like I was about to discover the New World of my career as a poet, and everything was about to change, change irrevocably.

I speeded up the first half of my transit through the keys so that I could have more time in Lewis's office, alone with Bly's words. But I was careful not to jog, not to go *too* fast, because the supervisor would read the record of the hurried route later when he pulled the tape, as would the client the next day. It was an old trick—to hurry through the keys and leave more time for sleeping on the other end. And though I did not care much for my father's business, I did not want him or the company to look bad. I loved my father and bore him no animus.

Finally, I was halfway through the route and there was Lewis's office and I went in, put the clock down on the desk, and tore open the envelope. On top of my poems was a notecard of expensive, creamy white, heavy stock paper, on which was written with fountain pen ink, in longhand cursive:

> *Don,*
> *Lots of energy here, not much talent.*
> *Best,*
> *Robert*

I sat there for a long time staring at the words, reading them over and over again; surely I was missing something and if I just looked hard enough I would see the more that had to be there, somewhere. But even after scouring every square millimeter of the card with increasingly desperate eyes I had to admit that no further message appeared. Then I shuffled through the carefully typed sheets of poems to see if Bly might have written anything directly on the pages, but there was no mark of any kind.

When I returned to the guardshack I tucked the envelope carefully into the beat-up satchel I used for books and papers, leaned back in my chair and lit a cigarette.

"Well?" said Don. "What'd cousin Robert say?"

"Not much," I answered.

"Yes, that's Robert. Either he's mute, or you can't get him to shut up."

"This time he pretty much shut up," I said.

And by picking up one of my books from the desk and opening it and quietly reading I signaled that the conversation was over.

———

One night during a shift at Pitney Bowes I tapped in to a seam of poetry and wrote a double sestina in an hour. It was one of those rare beautiful word storms in which the poem seems to write itself, with little effort on my part. I felt I was taking dictation.

Then I typed it out on Lewis's Selectric from the handwritten original, which took up four legal pad pages. Even at that stage the poem needed very little revision. I made three copies. One copy I left in an envelope on Lewis's desk, the other two I packed up in my satchel and took home.

The poem was entitled, "His Side/Her Side."

The next time Lewis came by, he asked me to step out of the guardshack for a moment.

"That poem you left on my desk," he said, "the one about a guy cheating on his wife?" I nodded. "It's *amazing*," he said. "I read it, and it scared me. I read it again. Many times. It's too real!"

"Thanks!" I said.

"And then after a while," Lewis went on, "I noticed the repeated words at the ends of the lines and I saw that it was some kind of patterned poem. Right?"

I nodded.

"What's the form called, the form you were using, does it have a name?"

"Sestina," I said.

"Sestina. . . ," repeated Lewis. "Sest . . . Six . . . —Six, yeah, six, I get it—six lines, six stanzas, six repeated words—yes?"

"You're a genius, Lewis. You figured it out."

"And now I'm even *more* impressed than before," Lewis said. "That's *some poem* you wrote there, my friend."

"Thanks," I said.

"*Some poem. . . .*"

We were both standing there, in the Pitney Bowes parking lot, smiling.

5. FINDS POETRY COMPANION

How Far from the Self • *A Little Help from My Friends* • *Ask Dr. Frankenpoem, Your Poetry Companion*

Working at a university where an immense amount of committee work is required, my colleague, Dr. Jackie White, and I have developed a practice in which we establish our own two-person committee, participating in what we refer to as "scholarship meetings" where we discuss and workshop our poetry. We arrange these meetings prior to the semester's start and post them on our office doors so that they aren't usurped by other responsibilities, thereby prioritizing our writing and establishing deadlines for our own creative work.

—Simone Muench

How Far from the Self

The notion of a coherent, stable, essentially changeless "self" extends from the moment individual consciousness clicks on, until death. Whatever else this *self* might be, it *is* an experiential phenomenon familiar to humans across all boundaries of gender, culture, ethnicity, nationality, religion, etc. It is an abstraction superimposed over all other categories, an abstraction that most of the time feels as solid as matter.

When any one of us refers to his or her *self,* the rest of us nod in recognition. *Yes, yes,* we say to ourselves. The two-year-old screams: *"Mine!"* We get it, we get it almost immediately—all seven billion of us.

Though we intuitively grasp that we are this bounded *being* separate in critical ways from the rest of the universe, the self appears to have no *material presence*—no locatable *where* within body or mind. It is the ghost in the machine, one that haunts us continuously, but refuses any summons to appear before witnesses.

Modernism took a wrecking ball to traditional, culturally limited, time-bound notions of the self. Ah, what refreshment! We drink it still. Postmodernists seem to deny the reality of self (or maybe just deny the word "reality," *sans* riveted quotation marks), and/or interpret it in political terms. Zen practitioners and others in various mystical traditions also assert the self's illusion, but posit a *larger,* boundless self, union with which is much to be desired. Strangely, postmodernists have no truck with their Zen ancestors; I doubt if Foucault ever quoted Dogen.

And the rest of us? Bank tellers, Home Depot employees, rock stars, nurses, teachers, roofers, cowboys, taxi drivers, the guy who sold you flood insurance—the vast majority of humankind have no interest in such matters at all. They know they *have* a self; *it's self-evident.* And that is enough.

Dear Reader, Dear Poet: who are you? Do your poems look like holograms of your self? What would it mean to your poems if they contained less of you, or more? Is the signature of your self in your poems? Is it good to allow your self into the poems? Can you possibly keep your self *out* of your poems?

It is all so confusing. And it is complicated many times over by emotion, by the fear that this quest for poetry we are on is silly, or at least that *our* participation in the quest is silly, and finally unnecessary. How can we ever be good enough? How would we know if we were? This rabbit hole, this hall of mirrors, this labyrinth.

And you, Dear Reader, lonesome traveler—like Clint Eastwood in a spaghetti Western—you lonesome self without a name.

Here's the assignment:

➠ Find a friend who understands poetry. It'll probably be someone who also writes poetry. It may or may not be someone you know well. But it will be someone you trust, someone who will not lie to you about poetry.

➠ Promise each other you will not lie about poetry.

➠ Each of you will write two poems. I am pretending to be your teacher now, pretending to ask you for a specific answer to a specific question. (In fact the assignment I'm giving you contains all the poems you will ever write in your life, disguised as two poems. I was hoping to string you along for a while, to pretend that this was in fact just an assignment, just one assignment. I do like to tease. But as you have gone to the trouble now to find a friend and you both write poetry and have promised not to lie to each other and are therefore so brave, very brave, I find it behooves me also not to lie. Even by omission.)

➠ First, write a poem containing *nothing of the self.*

➠ Then, write a poem made *entirely of the self.*

Arrange a time you will get together again, you and your poetry companion, completed poems in hand. When the time comes, lower your expectations, for yourself and for your friend. Meet on neutral ground. Maybe it's night. Probably it's night. Have a drink together. Make a toast, to poetry, or to something. Have another drink. Sit out on the porch like old friends.

Or, build a fire in the wood stove. Yes, a fire would be good, very good. Share a bowl of nuts. Maybe smoke a cigar, or a cigarette. Go on, for Christ's sake—one cigarette won't kill you.

Of course you will want to talk. This is your pal, after all, with whom you share the most important of all passions, poetry. There is so much to say. Talk first about the larger things everyone talks about—kids, jobs, health. Get them out of the way, the big things.

Now. Give each other your new poems. Read each other's poems.

After some measure of quiet, speak up. First one, then the other.

Say everything you see, everything that might help. Use all your powers in the service of your friend's poem, which is to say, in the service of poetry. Be honest, without cruelty. You are the kind doctor determined to remove every trace of infection, painful as the process may be. You wield the scalpel with thoroughness and pity.

When your friend speaks about your poem, sink deep into listening. Think of the poem as a child past the age of majority, getting ready to live on its own. Be detached, dispassionate. Be alive to the prospects your friend's comments raise for the poem's expansion, or compression, or sharpening. Open your self to gratitude, even as your words are being dismantled. Don't argue. Say thank you. Then, say goodnight.

Throw your poem into the fire.

A Little Help from My Friends

I am married to a poet and I think having a partner who understands this odd hobby and obsession is a blessing.

—Eric Pankey

When my poem "His Side/Her Side" was taken by *Poetry*, I was working full-time for my father as Vice President at Gleason. I was separated from my wife and living in a closet-sized room at the Stamford YMCA. The room, on the eighth floor, overlooked a downtown street that grew solid and loud with cars during rush hour but was otherwise deserted. The walls of my room were cinderblock, painted a shade of pale lime green, and the floor had thin but unworn carpeting. I never heard a sound from the rooms on either side of me or from the hallway outside. It was like living inside a safe.

My room was clean and had its own small bathroom with shower. Fresh linens and towels were provided weekly as part of the rent. No one talked to me. I could come and go as I pleased.

There was a Japanese restaurant just off the registration desk on the first floor where I sat at the counter and ate dinner most evenings. One night I saw a cockroach scutter across the wooden board where the chef was rapidly slicing a green pepper. The chef saw too and deftly severed the bug and flicked the body to the floor. Then, I was happy to see, he put that knife in the sink and plucked another from beneath the counter before finishing off the pepper. He never once looked up at me, but if he had I would have returned a reassuring gaze. I was not there to indict him, or anyone.

This Y, at least the dormitory part of it, had been built only a few years before and featured an Olympic-sized pool on the first floor where I swam laps for half an hour each morning. I would pretty much step out of bed, put on my swimsuit, sling a towel over my shoulder, and take the elevator down to the pool. I didn't even try to wake up, and when I slipped into the tepid blue water it felt like a continuation of some dream.

There was a down-market bar just around the corner where I did most of my drinking. The inside of the bar had a kind of quilted, stainless-steel paneling on the walls, like a diner, or the interior of the bar car on the New Haven line. Shots were cheap and the lighting dim. The atmosphere of cigarette smoke was so continuous and thick you could not see that the clientele was composed entirely of guys who had retired, from everything. Each sat drinking in his own darkly shimmering bubble of gloom.

How sad, I thought. I sat among them filled with pity. But in fact the reason I could see those shimmering bubbles was that this kind of place was beginning to be home to me. I recognized these men as uncles or older brothers in a family that had little to say to each other, but in spite of that kept gathering at the same place and time. And oh, I think now, as I could only feel then: there is comfort in the quiet anteroom of hell.

The acceptance from *Poetry* came printed on blue paper the color of pool water. I think even the envelope was blue. Beautiful. I brought it to work with me and opened it in private at least once an hour to read again the letter from John Frederick Nims, and to feel the extraordinary heft of the pages in my hands, a weight far greater than any equivalent sheaf of "normal" paper. There were printed pages of information about such esoterics as copyright and payment (*payment!*), as well as forms I needed to fill out and sign and return. I went through each black-on-blue jot and tittle like a Talmudic scholar.

It was a delight to fill in those blanks, even the thoughtless ones like my social security number, on pages I would later that day Xerox and take home. After taking off my shoes and fixing a drink I would slip the pages into a plastic sleeve, and then into a three-ring binder—my poetry brag book. Up to this point the book had been depressingly thin. But the letter from *Poetry* changed all that.

Now "His Side / Her Side" would appear in the same forum that had introduced Eliot, Frost, and Stevens, among many other Very

Big Deals, to literary America. These were my heroes. I felt honored just to be able to read their work, which I did again and again, though I sometimes read with an inner voice doing an interior commentary, a kind of PoBiz play-by-play: *Good line, Thomas! Good rhyme, Bob! Wallace, you knucklehead—where'd you come up with* that?

I loved the way the language of these giants echoed and played through my body. They *were* big deals, and I was no kind of deal at all. But now, in at least some minuscule way—the letter proved it—I might follow them.

Stephen H. came to my room at the Y one night carrying a three-quarter-full bottle of Bushmills. His head was entirely wrapped with white bandages and he was still wearing, unbuttoned, the blue shirt of his Gleason's uniform, his plastic name tag unpinned and hanging askew above the left pocket. There was, I noticed, a fleck or two of dried blood on his right epaulet.

I had known Stephen also lived at the Y, but somehow had never run into him. Technically I was his boss. It felt odd and awkward that he should knock on my door.

"Stephen, man—come in!" I said and stood with my back pressed to the bathroom wall to allow him room to pass by.

"What a day," he said, sliding into the only chair.

Then he paused.

"What are your intentions," he asked, "for the business? I know you love literature and write kick-ass poems, but what are your intentions?"

"You read the poems I gave you?"

"Sure did."

"What did you think?"

"Great, great. Great. And we can talk about them. We will. But now, now is now, and I ask you, again, because I would just really like to know, what are your intentions? I mean after your father retires. Will you take over? I'd like to propose that, that, that—that I be your number two man. What do you say? Well?"

He fixed me then with an intense, expectant, wide-eyed gaze, a comically large portion of the whites of his eyes visible. I knew, of course, that he was drunk already, that he'd been drinking way before he bought the Bushmills, before he even screwed off the cap, quickly downed a quarter of the bottle, and got it into his head to look me up.

Stephen was a drunk, and everyone in the office knew it. But when I signed him up he appeared to be a clean-cut articulate intelligent guy who had a BA in English from Fairleigh Dickinson. He had always been interested, really, he said, in the security field as a possible career choice and was curious as to what we could offer him, and he could offer us. You're kidding, I said. No! He had always liked the idea of protection, of using his intelligence to help keep people safe. Also, and to be frank, he said, he had discovered that literature wasn't all it was cracked up to be when it came to jobs. He laughed then and I laughed with him, in solidarity. I can get behind that, I said.

Selfishly, it was good to have a person in the office, at least part of the working day, who knew something about literature. Since graduating from Columbia, and then doing a halfhearted search for a teaching job that netted nothing, I'd worked in a totally male world. The topics of conversation were sports and politics, and the escapades of fellow employees at Gleason. *Literature* was *Hustler, Penthouse,* and *Juggs.* Intelligence was what you used to make money. What else was it good for?

This particular blindness said nothing about them as people. Many were kind and decent. They were working-class; I had grown up around men like them and I knew them. It was a world where you couldn't put on airs without getting called out, and then ragged, mercilessly. I liked this feature. It kept everybody from getting too puffed up. I would come to appreciate it, wistfully, even more later, when I joined the academy.

No, it was not a bad place, and these were not bad people. But I felt at every moment like an alien hiding his true status, trying to pass for native in a strange land. There was no one in the city, at least no one I knew, who was serious about poetry. I hadn't kept in touch with any of my fellow Columbia students. I was beginning to write the poems that would become my first book, and I had no one to show them to. It was frustrating, and dangerous; though I had learned a lot at Columbia, I still couldn't really tell what was working in the poems and what was not. When a poem was accepted at a lit mag, I wanted to ask what was it they liked, what was strong? There's no substitute for a tough, caring reader you can actually talk to.

Stephen was working with me in the office when the subject of Emerson came up somehow. Stephen started talking about "Circles," my favorite among Emerson's essays. His comments had real thought, real insight. We went on from there to discuss the Transcendentalists in general, and I told him about the poet from that period that most shattered me, Frederick Tuckerman. Stephen was interested. The next day I brought in my edition of Tuckerman's sonnets, the one with the Witter Bynner introduction, which I had stolen from a library in Brooklyn, and gave it to Stephen. After he read it through, we talked about Tuckerman—the grief in his sonnets, the modernist tone—how his work was badly underrated and ahead of its time. "They're better than any of Thoreau's poems," Stephen said of the sonnets, and I happily agreed. This was a singularity—a discussion of poetry in the offices of Gleason Plant Security.

For several months it looked like I had made a real friend. He even drummed up some interesting comments on my poems.

But it slowly became apparent that Stephen not only looked too good to be true but was. He started calling out from shifts, both guard jobs and work in our office. Then the inevitable day came when he showed up for work in dispatch completely drunk, and I had to send him home. In spite of profuse apologies and promises that it would never happen again, the call-outs continued. Some of his on-the-job behavior turned bizarre, and borderline. I got a call, for example, from the CFO at one of our clients complaining that he'd been having a nice discussion with Stephen about Hemingway one morning on the way in to his office when suddenly Stephen got rude and insubordinate. They'd been talking about Paris in the Twenties, and the CFO had gone on about how great it would be to live then in Paris unencumbered, like Hemingway, and just write. Depends on what you mean by unencumbered, Stephen had said— Hemingway was married at the time, and doing some work as a journalist. The CFO disagreed—he thought Hemingway had gone to Paris alone—but Stephen would not budge. The conversation became heated, and the CFO finally stomped off.

This guy's got a *problem*, the CFO told me, then hung up. I brought Stephen into the office for reprimand. I told him that in the end we have to avoid arguments with these guys at all costs. Just fucking give in. They were the clients, and therefore correct, even if their facts were wrong. We had to constantly keep in mind that to them we were instantly replaceable rent-a-cops, one of the lower orders of mammal. Clients paid the bills and, at least during the hours of our coverage, commanded the universe. We had to keep in mind that they took their superiority for granted; it was an illusion we could not challenge.

Later, the client asked for Stephen to be fired anyway, though in fact Stephen never committed a fireable offence. He just pushed the line, pushed the line. In any case I didn't *want* to fire Stephen. I still held some hope that the incidents were aberrations, that he would fulfill his potential and become a star in the admittedly tiny galaxy of Gleason Plant Security. And, yes—that I would have someone to talk to about books and, even, maybe, my own poetry. But like all drunks, wherever they may briefly perch on the way down, his golden days were numbered.

One day, I grew emboldened and applied to Yaddo, the artists' colony, and was given a two-month fellowship for the upcoming months of May and June.

I brought that letter into work the next day and carried it with me to my father's office. "I've got something to show you," I said and put the letter on his desk. As he read I tried to explain Yaddo and what the fellowship meant to my work and career as a poet and why it was important to go, to take the time off from Gleason and live with a bunch of other writers and artists in a Gilded Age mansion in Saratoga Springs, New York, for two months, where I would have a cabin in the woods for writing and a room in the mansion for sleeping and there was a pool and three lakes and rowboats you could use anytime you wanted, and where there were no telephones or TVs or interruptions of any kind, and where in fact a large, discreet staff made *sure* no one bothered you and another part of the staff, the kitchen part, fed you three meals a day and for all this absolutely nothing was expected from you—not poems, not money.

After I'd finished talking my father looked up from the letter and studied me a moment, his face a mixture of pride and bewilderment.

"Why *Yaddo?* What the hell does *that* mean?"

"I don't know, honestly."

"Strange word."

"It is. I'll find out when I get there. Let you know."

He swiveled his chair back around so that it was again facing me.

"Well, Butch, sounds like you've scored," he said. "Sounds like a good thing, for you. Go. Take the time. We'll cover. Write well. Don't screw off."

"Right," I said. "I will. I mean I won't. Thanks. Thanks a lot."

I met Sarah in the cocktail room, just off the mansion's main room, my first evening at Yaddo. We fell in love three days later. Yaddo rocked our courtship—no responsibilities, no interruptions, just two months of talking about poetry and art and falling further in love. One weekend John Cheever came to lend his name to a Yaddo benefit event, and we all got to shake his hand. I remember he was dressed in sportcoat and tie, and was charming, tanned, and short. We heard he got drunk one night and slid down the grand, Tiffany-windowed stairs on an antique sled.

Sarah and I worked during the day, she in the mansion's garden room and me in a small cabin in the woods. We swapped poetry manuscripts and, luckily, liked each other's work. At night we watched or listened to presentations of new work by fellow artists and composers. Or we played cards at a table in the mudroom. Occasionally, we went out to some bar to drink and dance.

It was like a little lifetime in heaven.

We made friends among the artists and composers and other writers. A bunch of us took to sitting together for meals; it was dubbed "the kiddie table." Some of these friends and fellow artists took part in our wedding ceremony when we returned a year later to marry in the Rose Garden.

When we left Yaddo, it was together, as we've been for thirty years now. I went back to work at Gleason Plant Security.

Now that Sarah was with me I no longer felt so isolated. But the job and the people of my business world were thrown into stark contrast by my Yaddo experience, and the sense of division grew in me. I was increasingly at odds with a livelihood that was, I saw more clearly than ever, jarringly distant from the work that mattered to me. Many mornings Sarah would tell me that I'd sat up in bed during the night and "sleep-talked"—yelling at Gleason employees or my clients. I drank, more and more. I drank every day, sometimes at lunch, always when I got off work, and into the night. I began to suspect that booze was killing me, but did not have the slightest idea of what to do about it. Besides, drinking worked—it enabled me to hold together in spite of the strong contradictions of my life.

About a month after our first daughter was born, I got word that Stephen had died. He was found in his room at the Y. He'd disappeared from our office, and then from our payroll, during the time I was at Yaddo. He was thirty-six years old. I asked around, but none of my fellow workers had heard from or about him. I read the obituary at my desk at work. The paper listed his death as *due to unknown causes.*

I knew the cause. Poor fuck, I thought. What a waste.

And then, as I sat there shaking my head with silent pity, I was visited by a strong, nameless feeling. And then, I could swear, a hazy spirit, one that made the hair on the back of my neck stiffen and tingle, began to form. Stephen had taught me nothing about poetry or writing. He had not become the literate companion I longed and hoped for. But there he was, nevertheless, come back to say *hi* after death—a pale, twentieth-generation Xerox of himself, suspended in the gray cigarette haze. He was silent, and held a piece of paper in his hand, which he solemnly placed on my desk.

I went along with the vision. Why not? I was not categorically opposed to the possibility of ghosts. I picked up the page. There *was* writing, but it was that damnable dream writing—letters and words that squirmed and reformed as I tried to read. Impossible. It made me crave a drink.

But I shook it off, and took up the work of the day.

Ask Dr. Frankenpoem, Your Poetry Companion

Dear Dr. Frankenpoem,

Can a bad man write good poetry?

Hoping your answer is yes,
Richard III

Dear Hoping Richard,

You'll be happy to hear that the answer *is* yes: a bad man *can* write good poetry. As can a bad woman, of course; Dr. Frankenpoem is scrupulously fair.*

In fact the truth is that the bad-man/good-poet has a distinct advantage over his good-man/good-poet colleague, as the former will have no qualms whatever about screwing the latter if it will advance his career, yea, even a micrometer.

Happy days,
Dr. Frankenpoem

Dear Dr. Frankenpoem,

A couple of follow-up questions.

Aren't you mixing the categories of "poetry writing" and "poetry career," as you have repeatedly cautioned us not to do?

And: Dr. Frankenpoem, who are you to label one person "bad" and another "good"?

Still Hopeful,
Richard

---

* For a complete list of *bad people who write good poetry*, send an SASE, along with check or money order for $19.95, made out to me, care of my publisher.

Dear Still Hopeful (Richard),

Good points. At least, one good point—the one about mixing categories. To this I plead guilty: I *have* in fact cautioned you to keep separate the *writing of poetry*, which is close to a holy occupation (or can be, *can* be), and the *career of poetry*, a wholly inferior and finally meaningless, though necessary, adjunct to poetry writing. The example I gave had our bad-man/good-poet screwing another poet over to advance his career. Screwing someone over is *behavior*, which we can see. Writing poetry on the other hand is an *invisible* process. My illustration sheds no light on how a bad man can write good poetry in the first place. Sorry. I'm afraid that I have no explanation for this phenomenon. I'm afraid no one does.

As to your second point/question/follow-up, *Who are you to label one person "bad" and another "good"?*—Richard, are you four years old? No, wait—a four-year-old *knows* good from bad. Are you a PhD? That would explain it. Or, perhaps, a megalomaniacal lunatic obsessed with world domination?

In any case, I'm glad to hear you are still hopeful.

Best wishes,
Dr. Frankenpoem

Dear Dr. Frankenpoem,

If you'll pardon, one more question. Can a good man write . . .

Yes yes, *yes*, Richard—Sorry to interrupt, but, of course—*anyone* can write bad poetry. Even good poets. Can, and do.

Now, leave me alone.

Cheers,
Dr. Frankenpoem

— § —

Dear Dr. Frankenpoem,

What about writer's block?

Sincerely,
Samantha Samuels
Wainscotting, IL

Dear Samantha,

Writer's block. Right. Got it. What about it?

Dr. Frankenpoem

Dear Dr. Frankenpoem,

Well, what . . . what should I do about it?

Respectfully,
Samantha Samuels
Wainscotting, IL

Dear Sam[2],

Oh, you want to know what to *do* about writer's block. In the future, please phrase your questions in the form of questions containing some sort of verb.

Here are some things you can do if you experience writer's block:

Write anyway.

If you write in short lines read Whitman and C. K. Williams and try only writing long lines.

If your poetry is generally accessible, try writing poems even you don't understand. If you write impenetrable poems, then read Mary Oliver and Billy Collins and write something even your Uncle Phil would get.

Write in a different genre. Write plays, journalism, creative nonfiction, lyric essays. Write a spec for a new sitcom.

Write "conceptual poetry." (Which you don't actually have to *write,* and will delight your academic friends.)

Write a letter to your spouse, your boss, a dead relative.

Find a book written in the seventeenth century only you find interesting. Write a series of poems inspired by the book.

Write an instruction manual, an obituary, a paper on composition theory.

Write an honest tribute to someone you hate.

Buy a magazine on ebay from the 1950s and write poems only with words found in the magazine.

Write a poem about your worst humiliation.

Write something, anything, you KNOW you will not try to publish.

—Or, don't write. That's okay, too.

Yr pal,

Dr. Frankenpoem

— § —

Dear Dr. Frankenpoem,

How do I get my poems published?

Totally,

Judy Wentworth

Warmsworth, Yorkshire UK

Dear Judy,

You know, Judy, of all the questions I'm asked about poetry, this is certainly one of them.

I have given a thousand answers, each slightly different, according to the audience and the person asking the question. Now that you have taken the trouble to write, I will certainly schedule a hop over the pond to Warmsworth as soon as I can, so that we might have tea (if you enjoy that beverage) and I can get to know you, and thence give you a personally tailored response. But, until then, perhaps the following suggestions will help.

1. Write *really good poems*.
2. Investigate the world of poetry magazines. Find some you love.
3. Send a small number of your poems, along with a brief letter, to the editor of a mag you love, asking that your work be considered for publication. Follow the mag's submission guidelines. In your letter, be modest and factual, and don't take yourself too seriously. Neither crow nor grovel.
4. Wait.
5. Wait. *Da-da-dee-da-dee-dee* . . .
6. While waiting, pray humbly for more good poems.
7. Write more good poems.
8. Think seriously about *why* we are here in the cosmos, and *where* we are going.
9. Receive rejection letter. Resend poems, immediately, to another mag you like.
10. Wait, again.
11. *Rejoice! The arrival of the first letter of acceptance! Huzzah!!* (This step is out of your control, and may come late. *"Late"* has no exact meaning.)

12. Write new, stronger poems. Get rid of older, weaker poems.
13. Repeat steps 3–12.

Pip pip, cheerio,
Dr. Frankenpoem

Dear Dr. Frankenpoem,

Thanks for your response to my question. I forgot to ask: how do I get my poems copyrighted?

Best,
Judy Wentworth
Warmsworth, Yorkshire UK
P.S. We don't really say Pip pip, cheerio *anymore.*

Dear Judy,

Yes, thank you for reminding me of the copyright issue. The dangers of contemporary poetry theft are too little remarked, and cannot be overemphasized. Here, for you and all my other readers who have sent in similar questions (actually, the same exact question) is the quick and easy solution:

Make copies of your most valuable poems (hell, why not include *all* your poems; we never know for sure which ones will be worth a mint in the future), keep the copies in a secure place at home, and then *place the originals* in a self-addressed, stamped envelope. Seal and send. When you receive this envelope back in the mail, place it carefully, *unopened*, in your safe deposit box.

Though this should fully protect your poems from being stolen, and will serve as legal copyright, it might be prudent to go on wearing your tinfoil cap beneath the Deerstalker. You never know.

Tallyho,

Dr. Frankenpoem

— § —

Dear Dr. Frankenpoem,

  What poets should I read?

Respectfully,
Bodil Torgesson
Husker Du, DK

Dear Bodil,

  A large and serious question.

  The short answer is all the poets you like (and there should be *many*, especially as you begin). If you are out there on your own, you can find contemporary poets online, through the many websites for poets and poetry magazines. The Internet is currently the best source for discovering and connecting with contemporary poetry and poets—by a long shot.

  Bookstores are becoming vestigial organs these days, and it pains me to say that I don't see that changing. But let me hasten to add: *bless* the few, the proud, the stubborn independent bookstores still out there—you are much appreciated by us poetry geeks! Keep stocking those titles that refresh the language with inventive beauty!

  If you live in a large university town there may be one or two of these blessed independents that still carry poetry. Additionally, university libraries will often stock a number of serials—literary magazines—in print form, as well as many books by contemporary (as well as dead) poets. All these sources will provide you with hours of enjoyable grazing, and you should make use of them.

When you find poets you like, go find their books and BUY them. This is the most direct way you can demonstrate how important poetry is to you, and to the universe. And thanks for the question, Bodil.

Vergissmeinnicht,
Dr. Frankenpoem

— § —

Dear Dr. Frankenpoem,

Who are the best poets writing today?

Billy Nazooli
Hoboken, NJ

Dear Billy,

I have my own list, but so does every Tom, Dick, and Henrietta. Some are better than others, but you will not agree with every name on any one of them.

I'd been reading Harold Bloom's ideas about poets and poetry for years, and found his insights provocative and trustworthy and, at times, majestic. Then he published his "best of" lists and tipped his hand about who he thought was good among living poets. Scanning that list for the first time—I remember the experience well—I could not restrain myself from saying out loud (and loudly), numerous times, *Really? C'mon Harold, steady now. . . . No, no, not* him! *Harold, dude, seriously?*

You might as well make your own list. It's fun. Just don't put any stock in it. Read everybody. Fall in love promiscuously. Be willing to change who's on the list at any moment depending on who you're reading or what kind of poetry you happen to need. Try at some point to figure out *why* they are good. Be true to those who keep making your list year after year. Build an aesthetic, with your own two hands.

Majestically,
Dr. Frankenpoem

— § —

Dear Dr. Frankenpoem,

How do I get rid of that obsessive voice in my head telling me everything I'm writing is total shit? Is it something that time and experience will cure or am I always going to be a neurotic poet who just has to write it and let someone else decide whether it's any good? I will constantly erase lines as I'm typing them because they seem stupid. I know this is terrible, but I can't seem to help myself! P.S. It's snowing here. Is it there?

Yours truly,
Heather
A Farm, TN

Dear Heather,

It is snowing here. But not sticking. Pretty, though.

Listen, if you and I quit writing or died tomorrow the universe would not shed a tear. Poets *would* mourn our death, but also be secretly glad there was one less competitor for grants, publications, awards, etc. Otherwise, the culture at large is perfectly indifferent. NO ONE can be sure what anyone's poetry is worth, or which poetry will last.

Given these givens, the truth is that that voice in your head doesn't know what the hell it's talking about.

Tell that voice of yours to *go fuck itself.* Tell that voice it cannot be in the same room as you, *especially* when writing a poem. Close the door on that voice.

Then: go on to the next poem. You have many, many more to write.

Hugs,

Dr. Frankenpoem

Dear Dr. Frankenpoem,

I was wondering, since I am having a bit of trouble with imagery in my poems, do you have some ideas, suggestions, or exercises you would recommend I try to help me with this? I have always been able to work the intangible in, but I feel less solid in making the tangible really sing in my poems. Any thoughts, hints, suggestions, or orders would be greatly appreciated.

Venlig hilsen,

Gretchen

Smilla, Sense of Snow, DK

Dear Gretchen,

I seem to have a few Danish readers. I am delighted, and would be happy to visit your country for expenses and a small honorarium.

Try this: first, determine the literal level of the poem (or stanza, or line, etc.)—such as "a friend's apartment," or "my room when I was a child," or "with the swans at Coole Park," or "a train station in Chicago." If the literal level is too ambiguous to pinpoint, try *giving* it a more specific setting, at least for the purposes here.

Then, write the five senses across the top of a piece of paper (*sight, sound, taste, touch, smell*). Imagine yourself back at the literal "place" of the poem, and fill the columns of five senses with at least two images each (e.g., "his bed smelled of burnt toast and aging cat," "her eyes black as copier ink"—like that, only better); the visual sense should have at least three images. Lastly, see if you can work some of these into the poem.

Wear your mittens,
Dr. Frankenpoem

6. AMBITIOUS FOR THE WORK

Ignores Outer Validation • Ink Runs from the Corners of My Mouth • Smarts • Things That, While Possibly Admirable, Mean Nothing for a Career • Things That May Move Your Career Forward • Things That Guarantee You Will Not Have a Career • The Pre-MFA Save-Your-Time-&-Money Quiz

Ambition is like love, impatient both of delays and rivals.
—Buddha

What is my loftiest ambition? I've always wanted to throw an egg at an electric fan.
—Oliver Herford

Ignores Outer Validation

Successful artists are ambitious. As a rock promoter said of a band he'd signed, "You could hear in their music the desire to be famous." Desire for immortality made Achilles a great soldier, and it seems reasonable to say that something similar helped make Frost a great poet.

Is that the whole story?

It's not even the whole story among poets. I've heard from a number of sources that the poet Thom Gunn, for example, seemed not to care a whit about his reputation. Even though his work from the beginning was gifted, provocative, and heartbreaking, the word is that he barely lifted a finger to increase his visibility, or his reading fee. Gunn is one specific example of a superb poet who took PoBiz lightly. There are others we can think of who operated in this admirable mode. And there are many examples of poets who, like Frost, were vicious competitors at the miniature banquet of poetry prizes, awards, and fellowships.

Frost was, of course, a major American poet. But the field is crowded with another type: the poet of modest or minuscule talent who tries to make up for it with a tsunami of careerist industry. These are the poets who routinely trade readings, flatter and befriend the "important" poets, start journals or jockey for editing jobs that will insure indebtedness from other poets, positively review books in order to curry favor, etc., etc.

But anyone who keeps writing and publishing poems beyond the age of forty knows how marginal the art of poetry is to American culture, and how, even if one achieves the height of poetic fame it is a *small thing,* in terms of trappings and worldly benefits. How small? Well, compared to the salary and popular recognition of even a minor player on a weekly TV sitcom, or an obscure lineman in the NFL, it is as nothing. Searching the general population for one person who can name the most recent winner of the Pulitzer Prize in poetry would be nearly as hopeless as trying to identify one specific atom in the solar system.

Why then are young poets so hopeful, why are there so many of them, and so many MFA programs created to answer their desire—more, in fact, every year? Why enter a field that promises so little?

There are cynical answers to these questions. From afar, poetry looks both sexy and easy. The judgment of its quality is highly subjective. Young people with no other discernable talent may gravitate to poetry because it promises the cachet of an artistic, one-of-a-kind life, the old dream of living on the pure products of one's mind. Also, and by no means a lesser attraction, the job of professor teaching poetry at a university—with its built-in modicum of respect, its cushy hours, its security in an unstable job market—all make it a sweet gig.

But the noncynical answer is that real poetry *is* the human sublime, and that young people see that truth. The young intuit (and can live nicely for a while on intuition) that there is more to our business on this planet than jobs and acquisition of the material. They have not yet begun to wall off their own souls.

And this is, of course, the explanation I choose to believe.

Ink Runs from the Corners of My Mouth

I have been eating poetry.
—Mark Strand

I was in the masters of psychology program at the University of Bridgeport. I had taken most of the required coursework, and was at the point of having to devise an experiment for my thesis work. This was in the early 1970s, when B. F. Skinner's behaviorism was the dominant mode in research psychology. He was routinely on the cover of *Time*, and as well known as Marshall McLuhan or Woody Allen. He raised his own daughter in a contraption called a "Skinner Box," in which every stimulus, and every reward or punishment, was strictly controlled. Skinner believed that whether one became a concert pianist or a plumber depended only on the arrangement of environmental stimuli and conditioned response. It was a radical extension of Pavlov's famous experiments. And, on a small scale, with testable behaviors and controlled variables, the theory worked.

People argued passionately whether Skinner's ideas were authoritarian or humane. His theory left little room for nuanced argument. At the time there was little debate in departments of psychological research. If you were in such a program and wanted to progress you did the Skinnerian rats-in-the-maze thing.

I admired certain practical outcomes of Skinner's theory. The fact that it actually changed stubborn behaviors that no amount of talk therapy could touch appealed to my streak of American utilitarianism. On the other hand, I had studied music and theater, and seen people with *talent* close-up—how they intuitively grasped complex ideas and translated them into performance, into art, and how they did so without strain or effort, without any apparent labor of "learning." If it was learning, it was a kind of learning without conditioning, or at least without a discernable stimulus/response. Skinner claimed that if he could control every variable in a child's environment, any child could be brought up to be a concert violinist, for example. But my experience, and my intuition (which counted for nothing in Skinner's theory), told me that claim was bullshit.

I was often asked if I was any relation to old Burris. No, I would say—*I wish*. I don't know why I always said *I wish*; I didn't, really. But I suppose everyone would like to be associated with someone famous, and I was no different. The easy cachet of a famous name was hard to deny; I was tempted to lie. I wanted to be liked. On the other hand, I also wanted to be left alone, and answering *I wish* usually ended the conversation. I felt myself wavering between these two desires.

After a brief though complete reign of psychology's kingdom, Skinner's idea was shown to be far too simplistic to account for the range of behavior it claimed to explain. Now I think only college-educated people of my generation know Skinner's name. No one has asked me if I was related to B. F. for years.

At the same time I was trying to come up with a clever rat experiment that would not bore the stuffing out of me, I happened on a book of poems by W. S. Merwin. I no longer remember how or why such a book came into my hands. I must have encountered it somehow through the university. But there it was: *Writings to an Unfinished Accompaniment*.

I read with total wonder. *No one had ever told me it was possible to speak this way*, I remember thinking, page after page. I had been a psychology major in college and a theater minor. I had tested out of the freshman English requirements. The last class I had had in English had been in high school, where Tennyson and other dis- tant, dead-as-marble monuments were taught, taught badly for the most part.

But Merwin's poems sounded a recognizable American vernacular—simple speech, but elegant and somehow formal too, elevated in a way I could not figure out. The voice seemed to speak directly to my most private self, without mediation. It was a voice

I recognized in some sense as my own, though it was a voice long lost. What it said was urgent, of the utmost importance. It was startling, and vaguely discomfiting. And yet the experience was also intensely pleasurable.

There they were, the same words one encountered in the average newspaper article. But reading the newspaper and reading these poems was the difference between a butter knife and Excalibur. This reading experience was real news, the news I'd been looking for.

Reading Merwin, some new part of me woke up. There was the excitement of ideas I sometimes felt when reading psychology or philosophy, but in this case the excitement was pure, unmediated, in some realm beyond or above argument. It was of the body as much as the mind.

I spent the next year reading poetry and evading my MA thesis advisor. The University of Bridgeport had an extensive collection of contemporary poetry magazines, and I spent hours and days cruising the stacks, nibbling here and there as if I were at some never-ending poetry buffet, pausing now and then to jot down a name or two that got to me. Later I would take out individual books by those poets and bring them home to my fifth-story walk-up apartment. Piles of sleek volumes became my gourmet meals, and I would devour them one by one into the early hours of the morning while nursing a beer and smoking a cheap cigar.

I read thousands of poems, hundreds of books. I had nothing to guide me but my desire, so I went from infatuation to infatuation. Later, after realizing that there were yawning gaps in my knowledge, I would become more systematic about my reading. I would work my way backward through the American and English "canon." But during this year or two when I first discovered poetry I read without plan, beginning with the contemporary, moving by desire.

The experience "set" me. I had found in poetry a substance that could not be surpassed, a discipline I could accept and devote myself to for a lifetime.

Perhaps six months or so into my exploration I began to write some lines of my own. Yes—"A writer is a reader who is moved to emulation" (Saul Bellow). I was embarrassingly proud of these little pieces of verbal junk. But at some level I recognized that these efforts were just sparks thrown off by an apprentice blacksmith. I was forging my first crude imitations, the byproducts of eager learning.

Such thoughts were heretical in the then totally materialistic psych department, and I kept them to myself. But while I mulled over them, and my commitment to the MA program, I signed up for Intro to Poetry Writing.

The workshop was with the poet Dick Allen. He assigned five or six contemporary volumes of poems. I consumed them. We read more of Merwin, and Strand and Sexton and Plath and Snodgrass and Lowell and Ginsberg and Giovanni. And we wrote our own poems.

Dick praised my poems from the beginning, which only fueled my newfound jones for poetry. There were others in the class whose work Dick also liked, and said so. But I knew his praise was not revelation to them, as it was to me. I began to see that most of my peers did not take whatever gift they had to heart. As talented as a few were, they would not go on writing poems after the class ended. They seemed to lack the ambition I had for my own poems, the desire to push as far as I could, to see if I could make something powerful enough to take its place among the poems I loved.

The most talented of us all was a woman named Susan D. She was older than the other students, but from my present perspective I see that she was still very young—maybe thirty. With each exercise Susan turned out yet another amazing poem; her poems were alive with music and imagination. But she did not, it seemed, much care that she could perform these magical feats. When praised in class she demurred, she pooh-poohed her poems. Outside of class she preferred to talk about painting, which she had studied in school and felt she knew something about.

One of the things Dick asked us to do as part of the class was submit to literary magazines. Susan resisted. No one beyond our class could possibly be interested in what she wrote, she said. Besides, process was everything, she had learned from painting. The doing was all—end "product" was a commercial myth. She was ahead of her time.

Dick told me privately he thought Susan was afraid of success. She was the type who could handle failure but not praise. This was a new concept to me. Getting praise for something I thought was important and cared about was *much* to be desired. Now I think there are too many people like me and too few like Susan. Everybody wants to go to heaven, nobody wants to pay the price.

Dick and I ganged up on Susan and finally convinced her to send out some of her poems. She heard back with shocking speed, within the space of the semester, from *Poetry* magazine—they would publish three of the five poems she sent. Susan seemed mildly pleased, but fundamentally unmoved. How, I thought, how was this possible? I was instantly filled with my first jolt of artistic envy. Already I had arrived at the point when I would give the top joint of my left pinkie to have my poems appear in *Poetry*. And here was someone who had managed to have this miracle happen without sacrificing any portion of her anatomy.

Thus my first lesson in the difference between *ambition for the work* and *ambition for the career*. I came to the class with the former, and, in addition to learning a great deal about revision and new poetry, and the Beats, Confessionalism, and other movements, left with the seeds of a new ambition—I began to know ambition for the career.

Both kinds of ambition would turn out to help (and hurt) me along the way, though it was a long time before I learned the pitfalls and ultimate uselessness of *ambition for the career*. But it was clear even then, I think, that my love of poetry, the passion I had to write the best poems I could, was markedly different from my awakening desire to advance in the "poetry world."

What was, what is the difference?

A poet ambitious for the work is struck mute at some point, generally sooner rather than later, by an overwhelming humility. Such a writer sees how vast language is—how wide the gap between the infinite possibilities of word combinations and the handful of combinations that make successful poems, poems that freshen the language and contain the sublime. Such a writer feels the monumental shadow of poems written in times past and sees the impossibility of adding to them, and yet forges a commitment to the task anyway. This is ambition for the work.

The ambition to stretch the limits of one's talent and vision while continuously checking the work against rigorous standards is both humbling and courageous. It is interior work—an "inside job"—invisible to others. It is work dependent on the gifts and character of the individual poet, but drawing from a source greater than individual self. Its aim is the *transcendence of autobiography*.

Ambition for the career, on the other hand, is temporal and explicit. It is work that at its best involves cunning, diplomacy, and skills both social and secretarial. At its best it keeps order among the files of poems and the records of submission. At its worst it features deceit, hypocrisy, preening, and the cold manipulation and disregard of others.

I stayed in touch with Susan for a number of years after our class together. As far as I know those were the last poems she published, maybe the last poems she wrote. She had been married to an advertising art director who worked in New York, and when they divorced Susan got her real estate license and began a happy, successful career selling houses. She had great taste and was savvy and charming. She also had an interest in architectural salvage, and in the restoration of historic homes. Once again she was ahead of her time. I imagine she sold a lot of houses.

The last time I saw her she invited me to go with her to an AA meeting. It might be something that would interest me, she said.

Sure, why not. I was drinking heavily, and brimming with bravado. I was filled with ambition of both kinds, but the lesser was the one that showed. I'm sure I had a number of drinks before the meeting. We went, and I understood nothing of what those inane, smiling people were talking about. But I thanked Susan and went immediately to a local bar.

I did not call Susan again, and she vanished into my past.

Smarts

It's rare, I think, to fall *in love* with a poet's work because we are impressed by his or her intellect. I *expect* poets to be intelligent, but I also expect them to take their intelligence for granted, not cudgel me with erudition.

There is afoot, I think, widespread anxiety among poets to appear *smart*, particularly young poets. It has to do with the near-complete embrace of a university teaching job as the poet's ideal employment, and the consequent location of most poets and things-having-to-do-with-poetry within academic institutions.

In order to get hired as poets these days, it's far from enough to write and publish good poems. One has to have knowledge of critical theory, and even know something of current research in composition. The trend is now and has been for some time for poets with PhDs to be hired before those with MFAs, even for those openings specifically calling for poets. It seems a bullying trend, on all sides. If I'm going to have brain surgery, I want my neurologist to be the smartest in the field. Yes, of course. But what does it mean to be the smartest *poet* in the library, or in the country? We don't go to poetry to be instructed, edified, corrected, or healed (though something of the sort in each category *might* happen), do we? I don't think so. Not really.

What we do go to poetry for is, in fact, ambiguous. And even if we argue that poetry does us good it's impossible to measure or articulate exactly *in what way* it benefits us. How poetry does add to our understanding of the world is, in fact, a profound epistemological question.

Poetry has expanded my idea of what language can contain, of what "information" might mean. It has been for me, through the reading and the writing, an instrument of contact with reality, a way of exploring the dimensions of that contact. When I am away from it for some time, I feel the world retract, diminish, drift off. Poetry for me *is* connection. That's what I look to poetry for, as well as a few choice other things, like delight, and enchantment.

But—*intelligence?* Where does that quality rate? Writing poetry requires the matrix of a certain amount of intelligence just to accommodate a necessary sensitivity to language. And it takes intelligence to gather and assimilate the poetry of the past, to know what's been done before and not repeat it. These are givens. It takes intelligence, perhaps, to recognize and produce the new. Intelligence in these terms is an adjunct to imagination. Granted all this, we could say that it takes intelligence to *make* a poetry of strong feeling, if strong feeling is what we want. Intelligence in these terms: sure.

Of course, we want the whole package. We want strong feeling, we want the *frisson* of the new. But, speaking of the new, what we really want I think is a coherent and specific originality. Newness is a matter neither of craft nor of ideological positioning. You can adopt a style or a school; you can't adopt newness. The genuinely new has a restless temperament and is congenitally dissatisfied. It is dissatisfied even by the contemporary norm of chronic dissatisfaction. The new is not cleverness of idea, and/or satire applied to the power structure of the moment. It is not yet another tired iteration of the blunt attack on the middle class. It is not even nonsense in its latest, most edgy form. Intelligence may aid in the expression of the new, but it is not the source of the new.

No. Originality is more strange, more shocking: it issues from a consciousness confronting its own irrevocable aloneness, just ahead of the present, as if for the first time.

Things That, While Possibly Admirable, Mean Nothing for a Career

- Teaching (unless it's at an Ivy in the Northeast, and you get to know Helen Vendler).
- Editing (unless you can horse-trade publications, in which case everyone knows about it anyway).
- Publishing slowly (worked only when there were fewer than seven thousand poets).
- Publishing fast (worked only when there were fewer than seven thousand poets).
- Being a good person (i.e., a good parent, friend, colleague, Samaritan, "professional"). In fact, being a *decent* human being won't get you publication in the local junior college lit mag. It may in fact be detrimental to your reputation.

Things That May Move Your Career Forward

- A job at *The New Yorker*.
- A job as the poetry editor at a trade publishing house.
- A job as editor of a hot literary magazine.
- Not having children. (The time & money alone. . . .)
- Being rich.
- An early death. Make sure you have completed the posthumous manuscript, hidden it somewhere it cannot possibly be overlooked, and arranged for a trustworthy literary executor.

Things That Guarantee *You Will Not Have a Career*

→ Illustrating your own poems.

→ Telling everyone you meet, *Hi! I'm a poet!*

→ Self-publication. Yeah, I know—Whitman, Ammons, et al. And all those articles in *Poets & Writers* on the hot trend it was/is/will be to self-publish. Blah, blah. I don't care. It ain't gonna work.

The Pre-MFA Save-Your-Time-&-Money Quiz

MFA programs are expensive, generally result in no visible means of support, and do not really qualify you to write poems. Before you decide to enroll (which I know you will anyway), take a moment to answer these questions, which may save you valuable time, money, and years of humiliation.

—Five or more correct answers means *Go for it.*
—Three to five correct answers means *Starbucks is still hiring.*
—Less than three correct answers means *Uh-oh—your parents were right after all.*

1. The only people who should be allowed to call themselves poets:
   a. Tenured professors of creative writing and/or critical theory
   b. Those who understand John Ashbery
   c. Those who do not understand Ashbery, but can write like him
   d. The long dead
   e. Anyone who has read at Open Mike Night

2. A sestina is:
   a. The intersection of poetry and mathematics
   b. Only to be written in undergraduate poetry courses
   c. A six-layer pail used to transport lunch in India
   d. Best written under the influence of opiates
   e. A very small ses

3. The median yearly income of a moderately successful American poet:
   a. Somewhere between that of a highly successful panhandler and a security guard
   b. Dependent upon the number of incomprehensible reviews her latest book receives
   c. A crying shame

    d. If you have to ask, you can't afford it

    e. About the same as the guy who engraved *The Last Supper* on a grain of rice

4. The optimal length for a poetry reading:

    a. Fifteen minutes if you're in the audience, a leisurely hour if behind the podium

    b. Three times the length of the poet's introduction, divided by the honorarium

    c. When the audience starts yelling, "Free Bird! Play Free Bird!"

    d. Five minutes shorter than you planned on reading

    e. When the poet can tiptoe off stage without waking anyone

5. Poetry is:

    a. An art

    b. Rap, without all the good parts

    c. A cool way to get back at the parents

    d. Da shit

6. Enjambment is:

    a. A type of smoothie

    b. An MP3 file-sharing program

    c. The place your cousin lets you use to have sex with your girl/boyfriend

    d. Some French thing

    e. Whatever

7. The last poet to win the Nobel Prize:

    a. Tupac

    b. Maya Angelou

    c. Oprah Winfrey

    d. Janice Dickinson

    e. Robert Frosty

8. The first lines of poetry ever uttered:
    a. Dark cave / pssst, wake up!– / see if animal come!
    b. He meant nothing to me, really.
    c. All things seem mention of themselves.
    d. I think that I shall never see. . . hey, get away from my
       meat!

9. The best reason to get an MFA in poetry:
    a. Last fun before law school
    b. No jobs anyway—might as well not have a job in
       something I love
    c. Poetry will save the world, my dog said so
    d. Supply > Demand = Opportunity!

10. Guggenheim:
    a. The German version of a wedgie
    b. A popular microbrew
    c. What to do for a person choking
    d. A part of the brain, thought to regulate naps
    e. Semi-automatic pistol favored by L.A. gang members

6.5. TAKES THE LONG VIEW

The Long View • *The Young* • *Family Guy*

It's taken a while, but I've come to appreciate the virtue of patience, or taking the long view of my writing life. As a student, I once went to my teacher in a panic, saying I was no longer able to write. She asked how long this had been going on. Three months! I said. She laughed, and said to let her know when it had been three years. Different times of life and states of mind will come and go. Some will yield poems and some won't. Leaving the field fallow for a year (or maybe even three) doesn't mean nothing will ever grow there again.

—Joel Brouwer

You don't need to write every day, but you can do something every day that connects to and sustains your life as a person in love with words, images, musics, stories, and what they can hold. Listen with the ears of a language thief casing the mansion. Cultivate concentration. As you move through the day, notice one thing that you would not have seen if you were not looking with the questions of poetry in your ankles, knees, and tongue. Remember a memorized poem in line at the post office. Read something of substance before you read anything else in a day. You don't need to do all these things, you don't need to write; only, on any day, do something.

—Jane Hirshfield

Individual poems come into being as a result of inspiration and hard work. But thinking long-range can be helpful. By long-range, I mean asking yourself what you want to work on and finish in the coming week, month, year, or five years. And then trying to arrange your life so that you can focus on those as-yet-unwritten poems.

—Elizabeth Spires

The paradox of art-making is that our miserable dissatisfactions are also the containers of the best information we have about how to make our art better. We are aware of what our poem-in-process is not—and we reach out with our minds for that very phantom to lure it, or capture it, or transport it down onto our poem on the page.

—Mark Turpin

The word "perseverance" appears repeatedly (in the Wilhelm translation) of the I Ching and that stuck with me as a word that a poet might do well to try to make their middle name. It is a useful fuel in the absence of encouragement, which can be fickle at best.

—Amy Gerstler

For me, it's about showing up every day: to receive the dull or mediocre, and when I'm lucky, what's really poetry.

—Andrea Cohen

The Long View

The jazz singer Anita O'Day lived a long, productive life, singing until the end. Two of the qualities that distinguished her from other artists, in a career that peaked in, and then outlasted, the golden age of the big jazz band, were her perseverance and her fearlessness. She could and did use her voice as an improvisatory instrument, jamming with the likes of Coltrane and Parker, and keeping up with them. Given the obvious brilliance of these musicians, O'Day had to be fearless indeed. This courage and willingness to adapt extended to the last years of her life, when she had lost most of her vocal range and flexibility, as well as her memory—she had to prop song lyrics on a stand in front of her when she sang in public. But even though she spoke half the lyrics, O'Day retained her preternatural timing, and her singing was still full of phrasing that surprised and enchanted.

In a documentary about her, the interviewer asks O'Day if she ever wishes she could go back to the days of her prime. O'Day, looking every minute of her eighty-some years—except for her fierce, alert eyes—answers immediately: "No, I don't."

We *are* the unstoppable process of the present becoming future, whether we like it or not. Anita O'Day recognized the fact, decided that she wanted to continue making art—which she knew demanded evolution—and *adapted herself* so that her art could continue.

Of course when one is young the deal is a breeze. Poets in their youth, in addition to being glad, are all about the cutting edge; they *are* the cutting edge. The natural enthusiasm of a body at its peak, the kick of hormones, the feeling of immortality, all converge, and art is a high. Anything is possible, the future fully stocked and limitless.

But what about later, after years and births and deaths and expanding responsibilities and disappointments—as well as the realization of one's own artistic limits—have been layered on? Poets are lucky to have a longer "youth" than other artists, especially those in the performing arts. Forty is the cutoff age for the Yale Series of Younger Poets Award, for example. At that age, a dancer would have been retired for perhaps ten years or more. Forty comes real quick, even to poets.

And how *does* one keep writing lyric poetry in the America of Lady Gaga, sexting, and iPads, after that fateful age?

Every (moderately) successful poet I know has taken the long view. What is the long view? Well, what it's *not* is a stab at the art, a dabbling, a part-time avocation. Taking the long view has nothing to do with a desire for the *cool* of being a poet, however that might be construed. It is not a decision to make a *career* in poetry. The long view is not an infatuation.

No. I'm afraid that the long view is a *marriage*, of poet and poetry—a commitment to a life with the making of poetry at its center, come hell or high water.

And if one *is* in it for the long haul, and knows it, it behooves one to behave in certain ways. Here are some of the characteristic behaviors shared by moderately successful poets who have taken the long view:

1. Keeps growing in the art

We all know people—poets included—who are stuck in some past, either their own or someone else's. They deny change; they close themselves off to new influences and possibilities. They may keep producing, but what they produce are generally slight variations of the same poem they wrote back in the day, *their* day.

It takes a certain amount of guts, *à la* Anita O'Day, to keep moving, keep experimenting, keep pushing the personal envelope.

I say *personal* envelope because one can't push anyone else's envelope. After the initial commitment, after the apprenticeship, after sufficient time spent intensely practicing the art, we come to understand that there are certain types of writing, certain tones and forms and ambitions, that are beyond our capacity and/or temperament. At the same time we learn what kind of things to leave to others, we also learn the things we *can* do; we sense the possibilities within that spectrum. And *this* is the envelope we need to be pushing against as poets—the envelope addressed to us.

After we have this knowledge, continuing to try and make things outside one's scope is a fool's errand. We can do so, and no one will stop us. Henry James continued to write plays after it was clear to all but James himself that they were no good. The great English playwright Harold Pinter published a book of "poems," as did the American playwright David Mamet—both were execrable. There are many such examples.

Perhaps they had some purpose; the plays deepened James' gift for writing prose? The poems taught Pinter . . . what? To stick to plays?

Early on, Anita O'Day must have realized she had the voice and spirit precisely suited for jazz singing; she didn't dabble in opera, or rock. What she did instead was to push the limits of jazz improvisatory singing, her form. And she discovered, to her listeners' delight, that she could make that envelope quite roomy indeed.

There are good examples of such poets in our time—poets who, while staying within their own instantly recognizable musical métier, keep growing, keep experimenting. I think immediately of Frank Bidart, Anne Carson, and Robert Hass, three poets with highly distinguished bodies of work behind them, still composing at the height of their powers.

But ah, you may object, *them*? What about_____, or _____? Sure, make your own list. It's a free country. While I think it's important to have a personal aesthetic, and be able to defend it with strong argument, that is not the same thing as *proving* the superiority of an aesthetic. The latter is just plain silliness.

So we have our poets who keep growing throughout a career, who, even as their mortal powers diminish, find new and surprising form for their gift.

And then there are the others. The stale ones, those stuck forever in some previous mode. Their poems age right along with them, and not in a good way, like cheese or whiskey. I could name some of these, sure. But, again, it would be my list only. Besides, given memory, I'd be afraid of leaving someone out. I will say that my list would include some poets who publish with "premier" presses, as well as some self-nominated experimentalists, who have been boring us all for years.

The literary world contains a rich variety of mediocrity. It is a wonderfully inclusive, diverse group.

2. Ignores the trappings

When I asked a number of my favorite poets to tell me what practices they had discovered that permitted them to write well, and to *continue* to write well, in spite of the anxieties of our craft and sullen art, the one practice mentioned by nearly all was a determined resistance to the "trappings" of life as a poet.

By trappings I mean, and they mean, those publications, prizes, awards, grants, fellowships, etc., that are intensely competed for by poets, and which add to a vita, to public status as *poet*.

It is easy to become obsessed with such things because, first of all, the drive for status is high in the hierarchy of human needs. People in every profession desire those honors that mean their work is of high quality and that they are well thought of within and without the profession, successful. Poets are no different.

Well, maybe a little different. The work we do is solitary, and in some ways antisocial. When we emerge blinking from the writing cave, we do so hungry for connection with, and validation by, others. And because of the nature of our work it is hard not to take such awards or their lack personally.

He has been published in The New Yorker, The Paris Review, *and many other distinguished journals*, we say in introductions to visiting poets—as if each copy of the magazine contained not the work, but the actual *person himself.*

The market value of producing poems wavers between zero and tiny. Poets generally receive little or no recognition from their immediate community—family, friends, neighbors. The cultural function of the poet has long been forgotten, if ever it did exist. Such factors only increase the hunger for what marks of distinction are available to poets. We want to be published in the best places, to win the best fellowships, grants, etc., because it is outer confirmation of our inner work, which is subjective by definition.

There is large temptation to take such honors as measure of our worth.

I don't think we can fault ourselves for this state of affairs. As I said, it's natural to compete for status. And a long, impressive vita can convince many people, inside the poetry world as well as outside, that the vita behind the *vita* is hot stuff indeed.

Why then do practicing poets who have done beautiful, valuable work warn so uniformly against attention to PoBiz honors? For two main reasons, I think.

The first is that such distinctions are based on inconsistent criteria. Trends come and go within poetry as surely as within fashion, though perhaps not quite so fast. A book of poems that this year wins the Pulitzer would have gone unremarked a few years ago, or a decade from now. Closer to home, the editor who loved us yesterday ignores us today. How to handle such radical unpredictability about the value of our work?

You must find your own secure ground, and ignore the criticism, and the indifference.

As poet Eleanor Lerman says, "[I learned to . . .] ignore rejection by literary magazines and other publications that I submit poems to because the rejections are meaningless; what does and does not get published seems to be based on what particular editors like, and I can't write based on what I think someone might like. I've learned to write for myself; if I like a poem I've worked on, then it's been a good day." And poet Eric Pankey takes this attitude even further, giving all poets a gift of cheering insight: "It seems to me an acceptance is the only thing you can read as a particular judgment of your work."

But the second reason experienced poets warn against the trappings is even more important to our purposes here. And that is, attention to one's list of accomplishments is, in the end, attention diverted from the effort to make better poems. In fact, obsession with honors is *corrosive* to the poem-making effort.

The absurd notion of a "career in poetry" is not made less absurd by "careerist poets," and we all know specimens of this breed. They generally spend a far greater proportion of their time ass-kissing than working on poems. The galling thing is that in many cases their efforts seem to succeed—they get the right publishers, the right grants, the right appointments. It's an old story, one not limited to literature: the good are ignored while the evil thrive.

But everything changes. Besides, if I'd wanted to make millions and have people cower in my presence, I would not have chosen a pandering life in the literary world. I would've become an investment banker. If my main desire was to have millions of readers and an enviable amount of fame and money in the "arts," I would've tried to write police procedurals, or romance novels. I'm sure that I would have failed at either of these genres, but if what I wanted was the glitz and renown of the writing life, then at least trying such forms would've been a better bet than poetry.

The truth is, moderately successful poets write poetry, and continue to write poetry, because it feels like an activity on the border of ordinary reality and the divine. Not all the time, of course. Not in every case, every poem. But . . . sometimes.

Nothing else I've done in my life comes close to those moments of exultation and transcendence I've had when writing, or reading, poetry. And I think most of the poets I admire would grant to their experience of poetry a similar level of gravity.

174

"Outer validation of your many accomplishments is not the point of an existence in poems," says poet Jane Hirshfield. "Altering the music and shape and comprehension of the real into some other music, shape, comprehension more real, undomesticable and unexplainable—that is the point."

Yes, Jane! *Word!*

Given this, of what importance are publications and awards? Vanishing, is the answer.

We have to find ways, when the world's blandishments call, to redirect our attention to the begetter, the engine of it all—the work and play of writing poems. There are a few concrete things we can do to that end. Or, not do. For example, we can discipline ourselves *not* to read the trades. I mean places like *Poets & Writers, AWP Chronicle*, and the contributors' notes of journals, and poetry listservs—publications advertising contests, calls for submissions, and lists of the recent accomplishments of our peers—which can't help but arouse our jealousy and bitter mutterings. Just. Don't. Read. Them. Or, if one is just starting out and has real need for information, to take them in very small bites.

Another way to conserve our best energies: we should early on develop an inner "businessperson," and rely on him/her to accomplish the paperwork necessary to a life in PoBiz—sending poems out to magazines and publishers, applying to fellowships and colonies, and so on. We should keep this inner businessperson strictly apart from the composer of the poems. In fact, it is best if they are not even acquainted.

This business of poetry should be done as dispassionately as possible, treated as a neutral duty limited in scope and time spent in the doing. It should be treated as a necessary evil. I will admit that when I first started out I thought of submission as a sort of casino game where you spun the wheel and mostly lost, but sometimes you won and that was a high. I kept a shoebox for the rejections, an envelope for acceptances. It was fun.

But when my publications began to increase in number and "significance," so did the seriousness with which I began to take the whole process. No more fun. Then I had to step back and send the businessman in, to replace the adrenaline-junkie gambler. It was a relief.

3. Gives writing prominent time

I work every day, no matter what. I don't wait to be "inspired," I don't wait until I feel like working, I don't wait until the gods are in a good mood or anything like that. I've learned I'm at my best in the early morning, so I get up early every morning, and on my couch at home or sitting on the train or wherever else I am, I work. Sometimes something good happens, sometimes not, but I've trained the part of me that writes to respond when I say "go."

—Eleanor Lerman

I started making writing daily a habit while I was a senior in high school. At that time I was lucky to have an English teacher who believed that a writer should, as he often said, "Practice, practice, practice." Sometimes all I do is doodle, change a word on a draft, or add punctuation. It seems the most important thing has been to set that time aside, with few expectations, except that I will be writing or revising something—anything.

—Mark Jarman

The Young

I think I've reached the age where it's not only forgivable not to keep up, but unseemly to do so.

When one runs into the older poet who knows the name of every hot young writer, hippest magazine, and latest movement, we tend to flinch, to shy away, as if from a kind of literary Peter Pan.

Let the young bury the young.

Family Guy

In the animated sitcom the hero's name is Peter. Peter is fat, vulgar, selfish, cruel, ignorant of any aspect of art, hilariously confused about American history (not to mention world history), and devoted to contemporary popular culture, about which he is something of a savant. He is also filled with an unearned, blithe confidence, and a hazily sourced but unshakable sense of entitlement.

In short, Peter is the new American Everyman.

This may be unfair. Maybe I should more narrowly claim that Peter is the American Everyman in the eyes of the creator and writers of the show, which is itself a wildly successful product of popular culture. But for something to be funny it must contain at least a spitball of truth, and *Family Guy* is very, very funny.

The show did not invent the avatar of American father as bumbling, inept, shallow, silly fool. That's been in place for a long time. After the wise and gently humorous crop of 1950s to early 60s fathers (*Father Knows Best, Leave It to Beaver, Ozzie & Harriet, My Three Sons*, et al.), the upheaval of the later 60s succeeded in demolishing the old father, as it did all images of traditional authority, and installing the new one in its place—the one we have with us still.

Dear Poets: Peter and his family, imaginary as they are, are the voracious, consuming cultural center of the universe. They *are* the mass audience. And like most in this massive audience, Peter does not read poetry. His idea of hell is to be trapped in a theater during a performance of a live play. Boobs, beer, and fart jokes— these form the nexus of his aesthetic interest. I don't recall poetry ever mentioned on the show. One can only shudder to think what revulsion the word might arouse in Peter, if, in fact, the fact of contemporary poetry has ever occurred to him.

And yet he seems to bumble through his life quite happily. Blessed by a severe and widespread form of short-term memory loss, the center of Peter's mind is continuously occupied by *the next hot thing*. As many have noted, these days the next hot thing changes with accelerating frequency; there is no time for sadness or regret or longing to accrete. Like many, Peter's slate is wiped clean even as new images are forming.

Appropriately, the images and obsessions that flash across Peter's screen are, like Peter himself, cartoons—exaggerated, generalized, reduced to base elements. Such ground is antithetical to the slowed down, particularized consciousness poetry requires. Even if one could somehow plant a poem in Peter's buzzing hive of a head it would be like introducing a palm tree to Antarctica. Poor, fast-dying palm.

In contrast, we may imagine a tiny minority of literary types who *do* consume poetry. This sliver of the American population, comparable perhaps to aficionados of field hockey in size and passion, is made up mostly of people who both read and write poetry. I am not suggesting their demographic doesn't like a laugh. They do. They *need* laughs, as much as they need their Zoloft and Xanax. In fact, many readers and writers of poetry are fans of *Family Guy. And oh,* they may think, in their caustic way, *if only the converse were true, and fans of* Family Guy *were also readers of poetry!*

Should we despair? Is Williams correct when he claims that "men die every day / for lack / of what is found / there [in poetry]"?

It depends, doesn't it, on what we mean by *poetry.* If we mean what we read and write, what *we* mean by poetry—poetry *qua* poetry—then certainly Williams is wrong. Peter is quite happy reading as little as possible. And poetry is high on his not-reading list. Unless it was some poem required by Peter's high school English teacher, who probably did not "understand" poetry herself and hated the necessity of including it in the syllabus, and communicated this hatred to the class. And in that case Peter would have been a shade happier still had he never had his nose rubbed in *that* poem.

Peter, I think I have established, is not *just* a cartoon.

But if what we mean by "poetry" is something more expansive, as in the generalized, more capacious usage of the word—"that golfer's swing is poetry in motion" or "that crème brûlée was pure poetry" or, the poetry of a country and western slide guitar or, the way a bowler feels the strike as the ball leaves his fingers, the vision of the beloved undressing, the impossible, sixty-yard pass that drops into the receiver's hands, the shockingly pure questions asked by a child—the list is endless, isn't it?

If we allow this definition of poetry, then, yes, Williams is right. People in and outside the world of *poetry* find the sublime appearing in an amazing variety of forms. That poetry is an immediate, intuitive grasp of meaning. It is fleeting and rare, but available. It is confirmation that some measure of grace extends beyond the visible. Once experienced, humans seek it out again and again.

Men and women *do* die every day for lack of that poetry.

In the end it is salutary to get right-sized about the place of *poetry*, the stuff we read and write, and to consider it as one particularly rich and complex example of a wider poetry. It has its own beautiful history, its own requirements and necessities. It is an art, an activity distinct from sport and craft and other engagements, although I'm not sure we can go much beyond saying it's an art that uses words. *Poetry* is important on its own, for obscure reasons, which no one has been able to fully articulate.

But, Dear Reader, Dear Poet: do not assume it is the only cathedral in the pines. Peter Griffin has his poetry, and he is very generous in sharing it with you: it's the poetry of silliness. We *are* silly much of the time; it's a good thing there's poetry in it. Your Aunt Alice also has her poetry, as do the girls in the mall, and the soldiers in the desert. Everyone has it, or is in the process of looking for it, passionately.

Sometimes the poetry a person settles for is not strong enough, or is a false poetry. We see the human disfigurement this leads to. It fills the evening news.

But this is not news.

Take a closer look at the poetry of non-poets. The non-poets surround and vastly outnumber us. You can't pretend they don't exist. They do. Look at them, hard, without prejudice. Try it: bowl a few frames. And if you don't look away quickly in scorn, some of their poetry may eventually enter your own *poetry*. It may widen the possibilities of your own work. This is always to the good.

The wider your powers of human empathy, the more human your *poetry*.

Take Peter Griffin, consummate American Family Guy, who displays relentless passion in finding ever-newer forms of *his* poetry—the poetry of boobs, beer, and fart jokes.

Okay, okay. He *is* ridiculous. And hilarious. But his search is not.

Acknowledgments

I want to thank:

Leslie McGrath, who was an invaluable help with both research and as sounding board for ideas in the book.

Sarah Gorham, editor extraordinaire (and so much more), who saved me from myself, more than once. Also, Caroline Casey for her superb editing, Kirby Gann for his innovative and dead-on design, and everyone else in the Sarabande office who worked with and on this book.

The editors of the following journals, where parts of this book first appeared, in different form: *New Letters, Ohio Review, Writer's Digest*.

Large thanks to the following poets, who responded with great generosity to my requests for thoughts on our craft and sullen art. Even if I have not directly quoted them in the book, responses from all these poets informed the best parts of *The 6.5 Practices of Moderately Successful Poets*. "Moderately successful" does not apply to them; each one is an extremely gifted and accomplished poet.

Joel Brouwer, Jane Hirshfield, Eleanor Lerman, Maxine Kumin, Mark Jarman, Eric Pankey, David Baker, Stephen Dunn, Simone Muench, Elizabeth Spires, Patty Seyburn, Mark Turpin, Sharon Bryan, Richard Foerster, Stephen Burt, Julia Story, Michael

Dickman, Belle Waring, Jeffrey Bean, Amy Gerstler, Cleopatra Mathis, Richard Jones, C.K. Williams, Chase Twichell, Andrea Cohen, Gerald Stern, Ann Townsend, Michael Waters.

JEFFREY SKINNER is the author of five books of poetry, most recently *Salt Water Amnesia* (Ausable Press, 2005), and two anthologies of poems, *Last Call: Poems on Alcoholism, Addiction, and Deliverance*; and *Passing the Word: Poets and Their Mentors*. Poems have appeared in *The New Yorker, The Atlantic, The Nation, The American Poetry Review, Poetry, BOMB,* and *The Paris Review,* and his work has gathered grants, fellowships, and awards from such sources as the National Endowment for the Arts, The Ingram Merrill Foundation, the Howard Foundation, and the state arts agencies of Connecticut, Delaware, and Kentucky.